重生

Silesia Rediviva
The Baroque Period in Silesia

巴洛克时期的西里西亚

波兰弗罗茨瓦夫国立博物馆馆藏精品展

Collection of Art and Handicrafts from the
National Museum in Wrocław, Poland

首都博物馆 编

科学出版社
北京

首都博物馆　书库

丁种　第肆拾陆部

《重生　巴洛克时期的西里西亚——波兰弗罗茨瓦夫国立博物馆馆藏精品展》

首都博物馆编纂委员会

主　任　郭小凌

副主任　白　杰　韩战明

委　员　靳　非　齐密云　黄雪寅　杨文英　杨丹丹　龙霄飞

　　　　彭　颖　齐　玫　鲁晓帆　刘绍南　黄春和

编　辑　孙芮英　张健萍　杨　洋　裴亚静　杜　翔　龚向军　李吉光

图书在版编目（CIP）数据

重生　巴洛克时期的西里西亚：波兰弗罗茨瓦夫国立博物馆馆藏精品展 / 首都博物馆编. —北京：科学出版社，2019.3

ISBN 978-7-03-060837-6

Ⅰ.①重… Ⅱ.①首… Ⅲ.①博物馆－历史文物－介绍－波兰 Ⅳ.①K885.13

中国版本图书馆CIP数据核字（2019）第047928号

责任编辑：张亚娜　周　赒 / 特约编辑：裴亚静
责任校对：邹慧卿 / 责任印制：肖　兴
书籍设计：北京美光设计制版有限公司

科　学　出　版　社　出版
北京东黄城根北街16号
邮政编码：100717
http://www.sciencep.com

北京华联印刷有限公司　印刷
科学出版社发行　各地新华书店经销

*

2019年3月第　一　版　　开本：720×1000　1/16
2019年3月第一次印刷　　印张：7
字数：120 000

定价：98.00元
（如有印装质量问题，我社负责调换）

重生　巴洛克时期的西里西亚
——波兰弗罗茨瓦夫国立博物馆馆藏精品展
Silesia Rediviva: the Baroque Period in Silesia
– Collection of Art and Handicrafts from the National Museum in Wrocław, Poland

主办单位	首都博物馆　波兰弗罗茨瓦夫国立博物馆
总策划	白　杰　皮奥特拉·奥施查诺夫斯基
出品人	白　杰
总监制	韩战明　黄雪寅
监　制	吴　明　穆红丽
责任人	赵雅卓　黄小钰　皮奥特拉·奥施查诺夫斯基
内容撰写	皮奥特拉·奥施查诺夫斯基　芭芭拉·安德鲁施科维迟
	赵雅卓　邵欣欣
展陈设计	李丹丹
文物管理	冯　好　李　健　闫　娟　李文琪　刘轶丹　王丹青　邢　鹏
	马悦婷　祁普实
灯光师	索经令　吕　欧
摄影师及图片编辑	阿尔卡迪乌什·波德斯塔夫卡　沃伊切赫·罗戈维迟
	埃德蒙德·维特齐　玛格达莱娜·维卢佩克　万达·波恰考夫斯卡
	朴　识　张京虎　韩　晓

首都博物馆
Capital Museum，China
中国北京西城区复兴门外大街 16 号 100045
16 Fuxingmenwai Street, Xicheng District, Beijing 100045,
P.R.China.
中文网站：http://www.capitalmuseum.org.cn
English website：http://en.capitalmuseum.org.cn

官方微博　　官方微信　　官方 APP

致辞

　　首都博物馆作为北京这座伟大城市的博物馆，每年我们以"解读灿烂中华"、"品鉴智慧北京"、"世界文明互鉴"三大序列举办临时展览。我们的"世界文明互鉴"主题展览尤其注重与国际同行合作，将他们的研究成果转化为中国的表达方式，让中国观众读懂对方的文明、感悟其他伟大民族的成长历程和对人类的贡献。

　　伟大的波兰民族与伟大的中华民族一样，都曾经历苦难，都更珍惜重生。1795年波兰亡国，45年后中国沦为半封建半殖民地社会。波兰人民在经历了123年的浴血抗争、前赴后继之后，终于在1918年重获独立；同样，中国人民经历了109年的奋斗，才最终建立起实现民族独立的人民共和国。

　　为了与波兰人民一道，共同庆祝波兰重获独立100周年，首都博物馆与我们的波兰姊妹馆——波兰弗罗茨瓦夫国立博物馆的同事们一起，策划了以介绍对方国家传统文化与所在地方历史艺术为主线的交换展览。2017年12月11日至2018年3月11日《晚明时期的中国人生活》展在弗罗茨瓦夫国立博物馆举办；2018年12月18日至2019年3月24日《重生：巴洛克时期的西里西亚》展在本馆展出。两馆的同仁经过长期合作和两次共同策展，都已成为友好伙伴，这是我俩和皮奥特拉馆长最为乐见之事。

　　两个展览都得到了两国政府和使馆的积极推动与大力支持，在此一并表达敬意和感谢。两个展览的展期都涵盖了双方最重要的节假日——圣诞节和春节，既是对对方文明的尊重，也吸引更多的当地观众参观。皮奥特拉馆长还与我们共同倡导在春节期间，在各自展馆里开展两地市民家庭的视频互动活动。2018年春节，我们共同带着红围巾，跨越万里视频连线。这一活动，在双方的正式会谈中，已被确定为两个姊妹馆的固化活动，将在每年春节期间开展。

　　中华文明追求"美美与共"，向往"世界大同"。中国国家主席习近平先生倡导文明互鉴和共建人类命运共同体。他在波兰《共和国报》发表题为《推动中波友谊航船全速前进》的署名文章时指出："中波两国虽然相距遥远，但彼此交往源远流长。"[①]这个展览，既是首都博物馆2018年的压轴大展，也是我们两个博物馆共同对2019年的最美好祝福，献给中波建交70周年，并以此庆祝中华人民共和国成立70周年。

　　我们愿代表全体首博人，并以我俩的名义，祝愿弗罗茨瓦夫国立博物馆越办越好！祝愿中波人民的友谊万古长青！

党委书记　白　杰

首都博物馆　　馆　长　韩战明

2019年1月

---

① 习近平：《推动中波友谊航船全速前进》，《人民日报》2016年6月18日第1版。

Address

As a museum in the great city — Beijing, the Capital Museum holds series of temporary exhibitions each year, which are *The Interpretation of Magnificent China, The Interpretation of Smart Beijing and The Mutual Learning Program of the World Civilizations*. In the *Mutual Learning Program of the World Civilizations*, we attach great importance to cooperate with museums world-widely, transfer their research contents into exhibitions, which help Chinese audiences get a better understanding of other civilizations, their history, culture, and contribution to the human society.

The Chinese and the Polish people have both experienced suffering, which makes the rebirth precious. Poland fell in 1795, and 45 years later, China turned to a semi-feudal and semi-colonial country. The Polish people finally regained independence after 123 years of continuous struggles. Similarly, it took 109 years for Chinese people to finally establish the People's Republic of China and gain national independence.

In order to celebrate the centennial anniversary of regaining independence with the Polish people, the Capital Museum planned an exhibition exchanging program, which aimed at introducing the traditional culture, local history, and arts of both countries with our sister museum — the National Museum in Wrocław, Poland. *Chinese People's Life in the Time of Late Ming Dynasty* was held at the National Museum in Wrocław from 11 December 2017 to 11 March 2018, and the *Silesia Rediviva: The Baroque period in Silesia* was held from 18 December 2018 to 24 March 2019 at the Capital Museum. The long-term corporation helps two museums build up good friendship and partnership, which is the happiest thing that we and Director Piotr would see.

Here we want to give our sincere respect and gratitude to the Chinese and Poland governments and embassies, as they have actively promoted and strongly supported the exhibition exchanging program. To show respect to the civilization of both countries and to attract more local visitors, the exhibitions were held during the most important festival of each country, the Christmas and the Chinese Spring Festival. Also, Director Piotr kindly joined us to advocate the video integration activities to the citizens of two countries during the Spring Festival, which held in both exhibition halls of two museums. Both of us wore red scarves to celebrate the Spring Festival of 2018 via video chat across thousands of miles. The video interactive activity is now firmly confirmed as a regular event between both museums, which would hold every Spring Festival after.

Chinese civilization pursues "cultures sharing among different countries" and longs for "a harmonious society". President Xi Jinping advocates mutual learning of different civilizations and constructing a

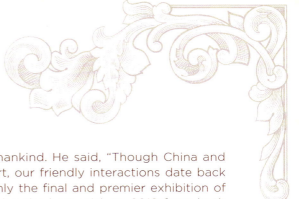

community of shared future for mankind. He said, "Though China and Poland are geographically far apart, our friendly interactions date back centuries." This exhibition is not only the final and premier exhibition of the Capital Museum in 2018, but also the best wish to 2019 from both museums. It marks the 70th anniversary of the establishment of the diplomatic relations between the People's Republic of China and Poland and the 70th anniversary of the founding of the People's Republic of China.

On behalf of all faculties of Capital Museum and in our names, we wish the National Museum in Wrocław a prosperous future! May the friendship between China and Poland be everlasting!

Bai Jie, Secretary of the CPC Committee of Capital Museum
Han Zhanming, Director of Capital Museum

January, 2019

致辞

　　展览《重生：巴洛克时期的西里西亚》的展品来自波兰弗罗茨瓦夫国立博物馆的馆藏精品，是西里西亚地区的文化遗产首次在中国进行展出，为此我感到十分高兴和欣慰。更让我感到欣慰的是，这个展览是我们馆与中国首都博物馆精诚合作的结晶。在此之前，两馆共同合作，已于 2017 年 12 月 11 日至 2018 年 3 月 11 日在波兰弗罗茨瓦夫国立博物馆举办了《晚明时期的中国人生活》展，展出了来自首都博物馆的文物精品。因为双方开放的胸怀和彼此的信任，我们才能向中国和波兰的观众分别展示彼此最珍贵的藏品。

　　《重生：巴洛克时期的西里西亚》展在首都博物馆展出了 17 世纪后半叶的艺术珍品，体现了这些珍品的艺术成就和永恒的价值。尤其是西里西亚引以为傲的艺术大师——米夏埃尔·威尔曼和马蒂亚斯·施坦因尔的杰作，在首都博物馆精心设计的展厅中居于最中心的位置。在此，我要衷心感谢首都博物馆党委书记白杰先生，他为我们馆能够举办这次展览提供了机遇。我还要感谢首都博物馆副馆长黄雪寅女士和邵欣欣博士以及他所在的国际合作与历史文化研究部。我还要特别感谢首都博物馆的共同策展人赵雅卓女士和优秀的展览设计师李丹丹女士，感谢她们为这个展览所做的贡献。同样，我要向弗罗茨瓦夫国立博物馆的员工——芭芭拉·安德鲁施科维迟、文物保管部工作人员和展览布展小组的工作人员表示感谢。此外，我还要鸣谢波兰中国文化艺术协会的芦雅兰和芦幽优，在我方逗留北京期间，他们为我们提供了很多帮助和支持。

　　《重生：巴洛克时期的西里西亚》展也得到了波兰文化和民族遗产部的大力支持，在此谨表感谢。

　　我希望本次展览会为中国首都北京的观众留下美好的回忆。这些艺术品对于我们——尤其是对于西里西亚和弗罗茨瓦夫的居民而言，是非常珍贵的。我相信，在人类情感和审美的问题上，大家的心灵永远相通。

弗罗茨瓦夫国立博物馆馆长　**皮奥特拉·奥施查诺夫斯基**

2019 年 1 月

Address

It gives me a special reason for joy and satisfaction that the *Silesia Rediviva. Baroque Art in Silesia* exhibition, showcasing works of fine and decorative arts from the collection of the National Museum in Wrocław, is the first and pioneering presentation of Silesia's artistic heritage in China. This satisfaction is made even greater by the fact that this is a joint project with the Capital Museum of China in Beijing and that it continues our collaboration initiated with *the Chinese People's Life in the Time of Late Ming Dynasty* exhibition from the collection of the Capital Museum that was presented at the National Museum in Wrocław from 11 December 2017 to 11 March 2018. Made possible by mutual openness and trust, the exhibitions have introduced viewers in China and Poland to the jewels in the collections of the respective museums.

The *Silesia Rediviva* exhibition at the Capital Museum in Beijing showcases great works from the second half of the 17th century, the achievements of universal and lasting relevance. In particular, the paintings of Michael Willmann and sculptures of Matthias Steinl take pride of place in the splendid modern interiors of the Capital Museum. I would like to wholeheartedly thank Director Bai Jie of the Capital Museum for inviting us and making this presentation possible. I am also very grateful to the Capital Museum's Deputy Director Huang Xueyin and to Mr. Shao Xinxin of its Department of International Cooperation. I also very much appreciate the contribution of Ms. Zhao Yazhuo, the exhibition's co-curator, and Ms. Li Dandan, the display's very talented designer. Of the National Museum in Wrocław, I would like to thank Ms. Barbara Andruszkiewicz and the teams of the Conservation Department and Display Department for their work on preparing the objects for the exhibition. I also address very special thanks to Ms. Katarzyna Matuszczyk-Lu and Mr. Youyou Lu of the Polish-Chinese Society for Culture and Art for their invaluable assistance.

The *Silesia Rediviva* exhibition has been made possible by the gratefully acknowledged support of the Ministry of Culture and National Heritage.

I hope that museum visitors in Beijing will find their encounter with Silesian art rewarding. This art is dear to us, the citizens of Silesia and Wrocław in particular, and we think that it also speaks the universal language of beauty and human emotions.

Professor Piotr Oszczanowski
Director of the National Museum in Wrocław
January, 2019

目录
Contents

展览前言

　　西里西亚，是历史上中欧的一个地域。今天这一区域的大部分位于波兰西南部，很小一部分在捷克共和国和德国境内。历史上中欧地区政权林立，战争频繁，地缘政治十分复杂。西里西亚因自然资源丰富，成为地区强权争夺之地，导致其政权更迭、边界变化不断。从公元 9 世纪到 18 世纪，西里西亚先后为大摩拉维亚、波西米亚、波兰王国、神圣罗马帝国以及普鲁士等政权所统辖，并由此带来了多民族的交流和文化艺术的融合。

　　巴洛克时期，是西里西亚重新焕发生机的历史阶段。当 17 世纪最残酷的三十年战争结束后，西里西亚迎来了一次"重生"：社会的稳定、经济的复苏、宗教的变革带来了艺术上的繁荣；而艺术的繁荣，也促进这一地区的稳定与发展。这个展览将带领我们走进这段历史，走进艺术家的内心，走进人们的生活。

Preface

Silesia is a historical region of Central Europe located mostly in what is now the southwestern part of Poland, with small parts in the Czech Republic and Germany. Throughout history, a number of regimes became active war players in acquiring stakes and interests. Confrontational relations among regions often drove wars, which made the geopolitics of the area even more complicated. Silesia endured being a critical battlefield for forces fighting against each other over its rich natural resources. Constant turmoil resulted in Silesia's borders and national affiliation had changed over time. From the 9th century up to the 18th century, Silesia had been under the control of Great Moravia, the Duchy of Bohemia, the Kingdom of Poland, the Holy Roman Empire, Prussia and so on. Nevertheless, the changes of regimes benefited Silesia to celebrate multi-national exchanges and integration on cultures, arts and, ethnic influences from various channels, sources and, backgrounds.

The characteristics of the Baroque period in Silesia empowered a renascent Silesian society in all aspects of life. The end of the Thirty Years War which was the most brutal and violent conflict between the Catholics and the Protestants in the 17th century brought about not only the religious movement which led to an artistic boom, but also initiated social stability and economic recovery. This exhibition is presenting the historical artefacts from the Baroque Silesia in the hope of that they could help visitors to appreciate both the common life of the people and the creativity of artists.

西里西亚政权变更（10 世纪至 19 世纪）
Regime Changes in Silesia (10th-19th Century)

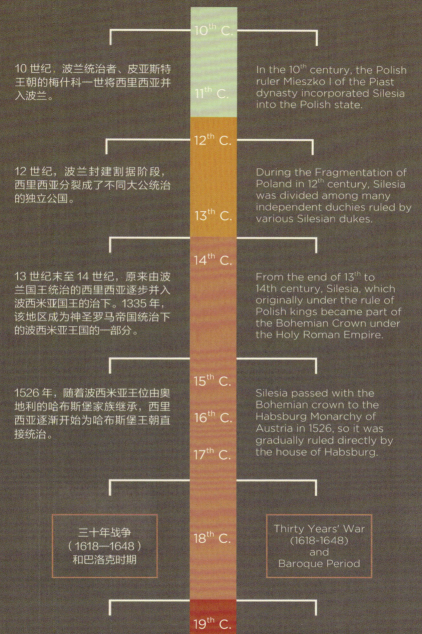

10th C.

10 世纪，波兰统治者、皮亚斯特王朝的梅什科一世将西里西亚并入波兰。

In the 10th century, the Polish ruler Mieszko I of the Piast dynasty incorporated Silesia into the Polish state.

11th C.

12th C.

12 世纪，波兰封建割据阶段，西里西亚分裂成了不同大公统治的独立公国。

During the Fragmentation of Poland in 12th century, Silesia was divided among many independent duchies ruled by various Silesian dukes.

13th C.

14th C.

13 世纪末至 14 世纪，原来由波兰国王统治的西里西亚逐步并入波西米亚国王的治下。1335 年，该地区成为神圣罗马帝国统治下的波西米亚王国的一部分。

From the end of 13th to 14th century, Silesia, which originally under the rule of Polish kings became part of the Bohemian Crown under the Holy Roman Empire.

15th C.

1526 年，随着波西米亚王位由奥地利的哈布斯堡家族继承，西里西亚逐渐开始为哈布斯堡王朝直接统治。

16th C.

Silesia passed with the Bohemian crown to the Habsburg Monarchy of Austria in 1526, so it was gradually ruled directly by the house of Habsburg.

17th C.

三十年战争
（1618—1648）
和巴洛克时期

18th C.

Thirty Years' War
(1618-1648)
and
Baroque Period

19th C.

1742 年，西里西亚的大部分地区在奥地利王位继承战争中被普鲁士国王占领，并于 1815 年成为普鲁士王国的西里西亚省。

In 1742, most of Silesia was seized by the king of Prussia in the War of the Austrian Succession and eventually became the Prussian Province of Silesia in 1815.

第一单元

精英阶层的重构

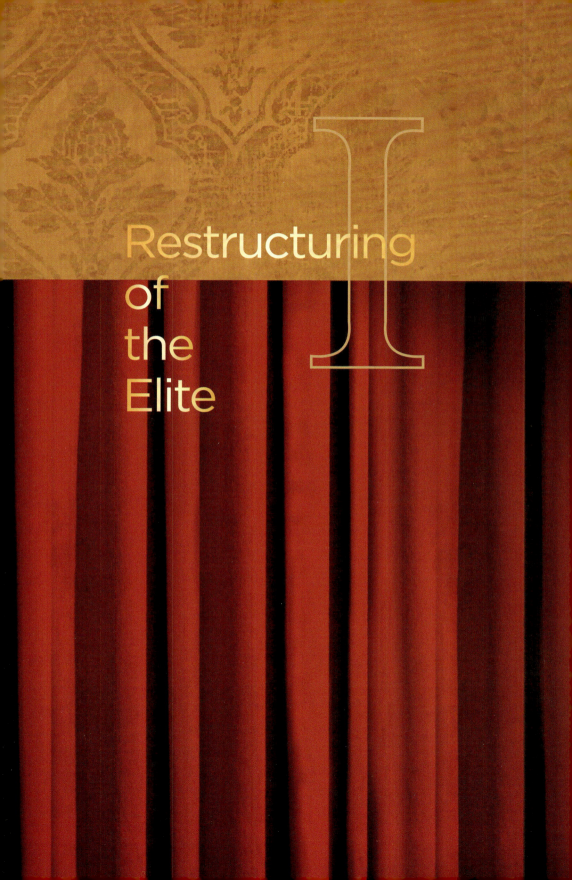

Restructuring
of
the
Elite

由于历史上西里西亚地区政权更迭频繁，形成了复杂的精英阶层。在 17 世纪，世俗权力与宗教势力中的新旧贵族，以及刚刚崛起的新兴市民阶层等各种力量在该地区角逐。

从 10 世纪西里西亚被并入统一的波兰王国起，皮亚斯特家族就统治这一地区。即使在被划入波西米亚王国和神圣罗马帝国版图之后，在很大程度上，皮亚斯特公爵们依然保留了很多特权，直接管辖着西里西亚。在随之而来的三十年战争（1618—1648 年）期间及战后，神圣罗马帝国皇帝逐步加强了对这里的直接统治，皇帝的代理人及其派遣的司库等政府人员间接代替皇帝行使权力，执行皇帝推行的政策，因此他们也是一方重要的势力。精英阶层中还有一类是新教贵族，他们大多来自德意志地区。早在波兰王国封建割据时期（约 12—14 世纪），就有很多移民不断从那里迁居西里西亚。16 世纪，随着宗教改革的发展，西里西亚地区改宗新教的比例越来越高，愈多德意志新教贵族来到西里西亚。此外，天主教神职人员也在精英中占有重要地位，除了已经扎根西里西亚的西多会修道院势力外，三十年战争后，罗马教廷派往各地的耶稣会等神职人员也成为精英阶层中重要组成部分。最后一股新崛起的势力是新兴的市民阶层，他们虽然在皇权专制统治下很难提高社会地位，但他们在城市建设和经济发展中通过创造和积累财富，同样赢得了左右政局的力量。本单元所展出的作品就是这一时期各个精英阶层的写照。

Frequent changes of governments in Silesia over the centuries prompted the structural change of the elite members who had different family roots and backgrounds. The 17th century was a critical period when the old and the new aristocrats, the religious and the secular institutions, as well as the newly emerged burgher class were all competing for powers and recognition in Silesia.

The Piasts played the role of the actual governors of Silesia since the 10th century when the area was incorporated into the Kingdom of Poland. The family was still in power even after Silesia became a part of the Bohemian Crown and the Holy Roman Empire with many of the Piast dukes' privileges and rights remained. However, the emperors of the Holy Roman Empire gradually increased the administrative control over Silesia during and after the Thirty Years War (1618-1648). Imperial officials dispatched directly from the court, such as the treasurers, were holding the executive power in implementing policies on behalf of the emperors. They were one of the few influential people in the region. Other notable powerful members of the elite were the Protestant nobility, most of whom came from German speaking areas. As early as during the Fragmentation of Poland (roughly from the 12th to the 14th century), the immigration of German-speaking people had already started in Silesia. In the 16th century, the Protestant community in Silesia expanded as the Reformation continued. More and more Protestant German nobles came to this region for settlement. Alongside the full-fledged prestigious Cistercian Abbey, the clergy in the Catholic Church became eminent within the elite group. After the Thirty Years War, Jesuit sent by the Holy See to various places also gained importance among the elite. Noticeably, struggling to improve their social status under the absolutist rules, the newly risen burgher class however became politically influential through the wealth generated and accumulated from the works they had been undertaking in Silesia's city construction and the economic development process. Objects displayed in this section reflect the elite from this particular time.

佚名画家
沃尔夫冈·沙施密特肖像

1678 年，弗罗茨瓦夫，西里西亚
布面木板油画
81 厘米 × 60厘米
MNWr VIII-1508

米夏埃尔·威尔曼 (1630—1706)
阿诺德·弗赖贝格尔肖像

1672 年，卢比昂日修道院，西里西亚
布面油画
58 厘米 × 46.7 厘米
MNWr VIII-2656

米夏埃尔·威尔曼 (1630—1706)
伯纳德·罗萨肖像

约 1684 年，西里西亚
布面油画
46.6 厘米 × 37 厘米
MNWr VIII–1180

Willmann, Michael Lucas Leopold (1630-1706)
Portrait of Bernard Rosa

ca. 1684, Silesia
Oil on canvas
46.6 cm × 37 cm
MNWr VIII-1180

Vor Gott und Ehren,
Will ich mich Nehren
Auff dieser bösen welt
So lange als es meinem lieben Gott gefelt

Ao 1654 Den 21 febr hab Ich mich Hans Ernst von
Wazensdorff auith Friedersdorff vnd Kuna Corrath In einem
gedachtnus abmahlen lassen, meines Alters 25. Jahr.

④ ⑤

佚名画家
汉斯·恩斯特·瓦恩斯多夫
和安娜·索菲·瓦恩斯多夫
肖像

1654 年，西里西亚
布面油画
192 厘米 × 84.5 厘米
左：MNWr VIII-3163
右：MNWr VIII-3164

Unknown artist

Left: *Portrait of Hans Ernst Warnsdorf*
Right: *Portrait of Anna Sophie Warnsdorf*

1654, Silesia
Oil on canvas
192 cm × 84.5 cm
Left: MNWr VIII-3163
Right: MNWr VIII-3164

 佚名画家
汉斯·恩斯特肖像

1690 年，鲁德纳附近的杰茨瓦夫
松木板油画
142 厘米 × 102 厘米
MNWr VIII-2476

Unknown artist
Portrait of Hans Ernst von Langenau

1690, Dziesław near Rudna
Oil on pinewood
142 cm × 102 cm
MNWr VIII-2476

约翰·巴普蒂斯塔·帕拉维齐努斯
丹尼尔·达特施奇
斐迪南三世皇帝停灵室

晚于 1657 年，弗罗茨瓦夫，西里西亚
纸本铜版雕刻
37.6 厘米 × 30 厘米
MNWr VII-881

Paravicinus, Johann Baptista; Datschicky, Daniel
Castrum Doloris of Emperor Ferdinand III

After 1657, Wrocław, Silesia
Chalcography on paper
37.6 cm × 30 cm
MNWr VII-881

 8

约翰·厄特尔 (1659—1726)
戈特弗里德·鲍姆加特
利奥波德一世皇帝墓志铭

约 1705 年，西里西亚
纸本铜版雕刻
30.7 厘米 × 38.5 厘米
MNWr VII-8351

Oertel, Johann (1659-1726);
Baumgart, Gottfried

Epitaph of Leopold the Great

ca. 1705, Silesia
Chalcography on paper
30.7 cm × 38.5 cm
MNWr VII-8351

利奥波德一世

Leopold I

　　利奥波德一世（1640—1705）是哈布斯堡王朝时期神圣罗马帝国的皇帝，匈牙利、克罗地亚、波西米亚国王，斐迪南三世次子。因其在对抗奥斯曼土耳其帝国的战争中大获全胜而一战成名。这场战争结束于 1699 年，大大削弱了奥斯曼帝国在中东欧地区的势力。这幅版画中展示了利奥波德一世葬礼的场景。他遗体躺在鲜丽的锦缎遮盖的灵柩台里，烛光照亮四周。画面下方，一只鹰紧握的涡卷饰牌上，印有一首赞美逝者伟大的诗篇。

　　Leopold I Habsburg(1640-1705), the Holy Roman Emperor, King of Hungary, Croatia, and Bohemia, is remembered mostly for his victory over the Ottoman Empire following a long war that ended in 1699. The war significantly diminished Turkish influence in east-central Europe. The print shows him lying in state on a canopied catafalque, surrounded by lit candles. The decorative cartouche held by an eagle is inscribed with a poem glorifying the deceased monarch and his deeds.

以下这些版画绘制了一系列西里西亚杰出公民的传统肖像，包括富裕的市民、神职人员和贵族。每幅画像下方都有人物介绍，并列出他们的头衔和职位。其中几幅画像还配有赞颂的诗句。

The prints featured portraits of illustrious citizens of Wrocław and Silesia: burghers, clergymen, and noblemen. Each of the portrayed is properly identified with all his titles and offices. Some images are inscribed with fragments of panegyric praising the man portrayed.

9

菲利普·安德鲁·齐利安 (1628—1693)
雅克布·林德尼茨
弗罗茨瓦夫医生菲利普·雅克布·萨赫斯·勒文海姆肖像

1672 年
纸本铜版雕刻
18 厘米 × 14 厘米
MNWr VII-9957

Kilian, Philipp Andreas (1628-1693); Lindnitz, Jacob
Portrait of doctor Philipp Jacob Sachs a Löwenheim

1672
Chalcography on paper
18 cm × 14 cm
MNWr VII-9957

10 菲利普·安德鲁·齐利安 (1628—1693)
乔治·舒尔茨
弗罗茨瓦夫议员库伯福尔伯格的西吉斯蒙德侯爵肖像

17 世纪后半叶，西里西亚
纸本铜版雕刻
28 厘米 × 17.5 厘米
MNWr VII-929

Kilian, Philip (1628-1693); Schulz, Georg

Portrait of councilman Sigismund Fürst von Kupferberg

Second half of the 17th century, Silesia
Chalcography on paper
28 cm × 17.5 cm
MNWr VII-929

菲利普·安德鲁·齐利安 (1628—1693)
乔治·舒尔茨

议员及司库约翰尼斯·哥兹肖像

17 世纪后半叶，西里西亚
纸本铜版雕刻
27.5 厘米 × 17.5 厘米
MNWr VII-925

Kilian, Philip (1628-1693); Schulz, Georg
Portrait of councilman and treasurer Johannes Gotz

Second half of the 17th century, Silesia
Chalcography on paper
27.5 cm × 17.5 cm
MNWr VII-925

菲利普·安德鲁·齐利安 (1628—1693)
乔治·舒尔茨

弗罗茨瓦夫议员大卫·冯·伊比恩·史特拉西维兹肖像

17 世纪后半叶，西里西亚
纸本铜版雕刻
27.5 厘米 × 17.4 厘米
MNWr VII–912

Kilian, Philip (1628-1693); Schulz, Georg

Portrait of Wrocław councilman David von Eben auf Strachwitz

Second half of the 17th century, Silesia
Chalcography on paper
27.5 cm × 17.4 cm
MNWr VII–912

菲利普·安德鲁·齐利安 (1628—1693)
乔治·舒尔茨
弗罗茨瓦夫议员约翰·西吉斯蒙德·豪纳尔德肖像

17 世纪后半叶，西里西亚
纸本铜版雕刻
28 厘米 × 17.5 厘米
MNWr VII-926

Kilian, Philip (1628-1693); Schulz, Georg
Portrait of Wrocław councilman Johann Sigismund Haunold

Second half of the 17th century, Silesia
Chalcography on paper
28 cm x 17.5 cm
MNWr VII-926

13

菲利普·安德鲁·齐利安 (1628—1693)
乔治·舒尔茨

牧师约翰尼斯·阿库鲁图斯肖像

1669 年，弗罗茨瓦夫，西里西亚
纸本铜版雕刻
32 厘米 × 23.5 厘米
MNWr VII–4719

Kilian, Philip (1628-1693); Schulz, Georg

Portrait of pastor Johannes Akolut

1669, Wrocław, Silesia
Chalcography on paper
32 cm × 23.5 cm
MNWr VII-4719

菲利普 · 安德鲁 · 齐利安 (1628—1693)
乔治 · 舒尔茨

牧师米夏埃尔 · 海尔曼肖像

1667 年，弗罗茨瓦夫，西里西亚
纸本铜版雕刻
32.3 厘米 × 20.5 厘米
MNWr VII-5109

Kilian, Philip (1628-1693); Schulz, Georg
Portrait of pastor Michael Hermann

1667, Wrocław, Silesia
Chalcography on paper
32.3 cm × 20.5 cm
MNWr VII-5109

约翰 · 厄特尔 (1659—1726)

男爵西吉斯蒙德·海因里希肖像

17 世纪末制版，20 世纪印制，西里西亚
纸本铜版雕刻
30 厘米 × 20 厘米
MNWr VII–12975

Oertel, Johann (1659-1726)

Portrait of baron Sigismund Heinrich von Biebran

Second half of the 17th century (print from 20th century), Silesia
Chalcography on paper
30 cm × 20 cm
MNWr VII–12975

约翰·厄特尔 (1659—1726)
希维德尼察公国的贵族沙夫高士伯爵克里斯托弗·利奥波德肖像

17 世纪末制版，20 世纪印制，西里西亚
纸本铜版雕刻
23.5 厘米 × 15.7 厘米
MNWr VII-876/3

Oertel, Johann (1659-1726)

Portrait of starost of Świdnica Duchy,
Christophor Leopold count von Schafgotsch

Second half of the 17th century (print from 20th century), Silesia
Chalcography on paper
23.5 cm × 15.7 cm
MNWr VII-876/3

第二单元
巴洛克艺术的兴盛

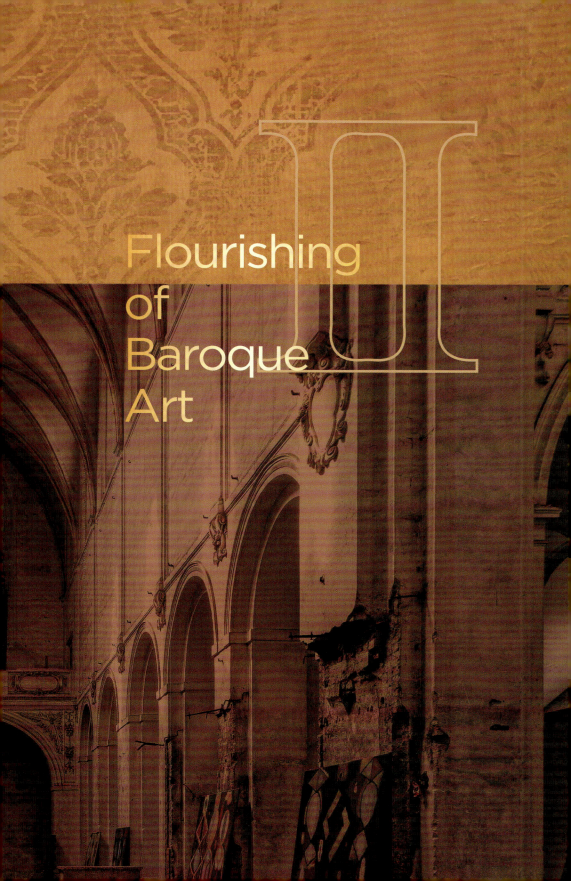

Flourishing of Baroque Art

II

　　巴洛克艺术起源于16世纪中叶的意大利，兴盛于整个17世纪。相比之下，西里西亚的巴洛克时代晚了将近1个世纪。其主要原因是成为三十年战争主战场的西里西亚遭受了重创，城市破败、民生凋敝，社会发展停滞不前。然而也正是这场战争的结果，使西里西亚迎来了艺术发展的重要转折点：首先，曾经新教占主导的西里西亚地区重新回到天主教教会的控制之下；其次，由于其地理位置靠近中欧地区两个重要的巴洛克艺术中心——奥地利的维也纳和波西米亚的布拉格，那里是信奉天主教的神圣罗马帝国皇帝的世袭领地。当推崇张扬、惊艳和激情的巴洛克艺术的天主教代替了崇尚简朴和简约的新教，曾经默默无闻的西里西亚艺术进入了新的繁荣时期。

　　画家米夏埃尔·威尔曼和雕塑家马蒂亚斯·施坦因尔承担了这一使命，他们非凡的创作丰富了人们的生活。这些作品充满了想象力和艺术感染力，受到广泛的赞誉。他们也由此被视为西里西亚巴洛克艺术史上最杰出的人物。

The Baroque originated from Italy in the mid-16th century, and flourished through the entire 17th century. It arrived in Silesia nearly a century later due to instability caused by wars. Being a primary war zone during the Thirty Years War, Silesia had suffered heavy losses. Cities were sabotaged, most people lived in poverty, and the stagnation in social development was holding the cultural recovery back. However, the results of this war provided opportunities for the turning point for artistic development in Silesia: firstly, Silesia was once again back under the control of the Catholic Churches; and secondly, Silesia was, geographically, close to two Baroque art centers: Vienna in Austria and Prague in Bohemia — the domains of the Holy Roman Emperors. Being in this location had a significant impact on art in Silesia during the Baroque period. When the Catholic establishments replaced the Protestant churches, the reserved, simple-formed art was also substituted by the imaginative, passionate and, flamboyant Baroque art. It was when the shaded Silesian art stepped into the limelight and flourish.

Michael Lucas Leopold Willmann, the painter, and Matthias Steinl, the sculptor were the two great artists who stood out representing the highest achievement of early Baroque art in Silesia. They devoted their lives to the creation of artwork for churches and the public, and have gained worldwide appreciation and recognition by their masterpieces of imagination and artistic inspirations. Therefore, they were the most renowned Baroque figures in the Silesian art history.

第一节

画家米夏埃尔·利奥波德·威尔曼
Michael Leopold Willmann

米夏埃尔·利奥波德·威尔曼（1630—1706）是在西里西亚地区工作生活过的最杰出的巴洛克风格画家。他出生于普鲁士的哥尼斯堡（今俄罗斯加里宁格勒市），曾前往荷兰、格但斯克、柏林和布拉格等地学习绘画，特别是曾造访了荷兰阿姆斯特丹的著名画家伦勃朗的工作室。在那里他获得了很多灵感和启发。后来他长期定居西里西亚，几乎从未离开。他的作品主要以宗教主题为主，大多为卢比昂日、克热舒夫等地的西多会修道院创作。除了大型油画作品和肖像画外，晚年还创作多幅巨制的天顶壁画。在这里我们集中展出了他的多种不同题材作品，既有肖像、神话题材，也有宗教题材，全面展现他不同的艺术风格。第一单元中的《伯纳德·罗萨肖像》和《阿诺德·弗赖贝格尔肖像》也是其肖像画的杰作。强烈的明暗对比，栩栩如生的形象刻画，使其肖像画一点也不逊色于荷兰的大师作品。

Michael Leopold Willmann (1630-1706) was the most distinguished Baroque painter who worked in Silesia. The artist was born in Królewiec; in his youth, he made some study trips to Holland (while in Amsterdam he even visited the studio of Rembrandt himself), Gdańsk, Berlin and Prague, and finally settled in Silesia. He spent there the rest of his life, painting mostly religious pictures commissioned by the abbots of the Cistercian monasteries in Lubiąż and Krzeszów. He also created a number of giant ceiling murals in later years of his life. In this exhibition, we present his works on various subjects, including portraits, myths and religions, showing his different artistic styles in an all-round way.

18

米夏埃尔·威尔曼 (1630—1706)
自画像

1682 年，卢比昂日修道院，西里西亚
布面油画
64.5 厘米 × 51.5 厘米
MNWr VIII-3149

Willmann, Michael Lucas Leopold
(1630-1706)

Self- portrait

1682, Lubiąż Abbey, Silesia
Oil on canvas
64.5 cm × 51.5 cm
MNWr VIII-3149

 米夏埃尔·威尔曼（1630—1706）
俄耳甫斯为动物演奏音乐

约 1670 年，卢比昂日修道院，西里西亚
布面油画
112 厘米 × 144 厘米
MNWr VIII-667

Willmann, Michael Lucas Leopold (1630-1706)
Orpheus playing music for the animals

ca. 1670, Lubiąż Abbey, Silesia
Oil on canvas
112 cm × 144 cm
MNWr VIII-667

米夏埃尔・威尔曼 (1630—1706)
绑架珀尔塞福涅

约 1665 年，西里西亚
布面油画
121 厘米 × 172 厘米
MNWr VIII-666

Willmann, Michael Lucas Leopold (1630-1706)
The Abduction of Persephone

ca. 1665, Silesia
Oil on canvas
121 cm × 172 cm
MNWr VIII-666

米夏埃尔·威尔曼 (1630—1706)
逃往埃及

约 1685 年，卢比昂日修道院，西里西亚
布面油画
163 厘米 × 198 厘米
MNWr VIII-2658

Willmann, Michael Lucas Leopold (1630-1706)
The Flight into Egypt

ca. 1685, Lubiąż Abbey, Silesia
Oil on canvas
163 cm × 198 cm
MNWr VIII-2658

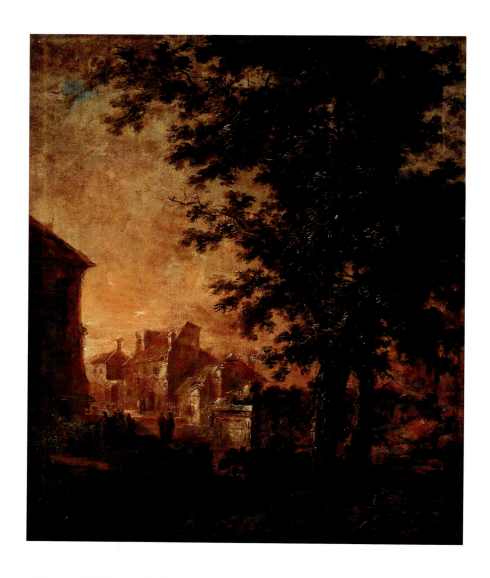

22 米夏埃尔·威尔曼 (1630—1706)
召唤圣马太

约 1675 年，卢比昂日修道院，西里西亚
布面油画
107 厘米 × 87.5 厘米
MNWr VIII-3198

Willmann, Michael Lucas Leopold (1630-1706)
The Calling of St. Matthew

ca. 1675, Lubiąż Abbey, Silesia
Oil on canvas
107 cm × 87.5 cm
MNWr VIII-3198

米夏埃尔·威尔曼 (1630—1706)
圣凯瑟琳

约 1690 年，西里西亚
布面油画
50 厘米 × 35.7 厘米
MNWr VIII-2635c

Willmann, Michael Lucas Leopold (1630-1706)
Saint Catherine

ca. 1690, Silesia
Oil or canvas
50 cm × 35.7 cm
MNWr VIII-2635c

米夏埃尔 · 威尔曼 (1630—1706)
圣莫妮卡

1660—1670 年，西里西亚
云杉木板油画
84 厘米 × 64 厘米
MNWr VIII-550

Willmann, Michael Lucas Leopold (1630-1706)
Saint Monica

1660-1670, Silesia
Oil on spruce
84 cm × 64 cm
MNWr VIII-550

 25

米夏埃尔·威尔曼 (1630—1706)
圣乌尔苏拉

约 1685 年, 西里西亚
布面油画
186 厘米 × 116 厘米
MNWr VIII-3154

Willmann, Michael Lucas Leopold (1630-1706)
Saint Ursula

ca. 1685, Silesia
Oil on canvas
186 cm × 116 cm
MNWr VIII-3154

第二节

雕塑家马蒂亚斯·施坦因尔

Matthias Steinl

马蒂亚斯·施坦因尔（约 1644—1727）可能出生于今奥地利萨尔茨堡附近，是巴洛克风格的重要建筑师和雕塑家之一。他于 1676 年接受了当时卢比昂日的修道院院长约翰·赖希的提议来到西里西亚，并生活在卢比昂日直到 1682 年。他为修道院的教堂创造了众多艺术品，例如侧祭坛、主祭坛（与米夏埃尔·威尔曼合作），以及天使唱诗班座椅等。1682 年，施坦因尔搬到了距离卢比昂日 40 多千米的弗罗茨瓦夫，居住在座堂岛（又称大教堂岛），为主教工作。虽然他于 1687 年离开弗罗茨瓦夫前往维也纳（今奥地利首都），成为神圣罗马帝国的皇家御用雕刻家和版画家，但他继续为弗罗茨瓦夫的教堂设计了主祭坛（1715 年）。

Matthias Steinl (ca. 1644 – 1727) probably was one of the best known sculptor and architect, who originated from the area round Salzburg. He came to Silesia in 1676 at the initiative of Johann Reich, then abbot of the Cistersian Abbey in Lubiąż. He stayed in Lubiąż until 1682. There he created many pieces of art for the abbey church: the side altars, the main altar and so-called the angelic choir stalls. In 1682 Steinl moved to Wrocław (he lived at Ostrów Tumski – The Cathedral Island) and worked for the bishop. In 1687 Steinl became a court sculptor and printmaker at the emperor's court in Vienna, but he also designed the main altar for a church in Wrocław (1715).

卢比昂日修道院教堂的今昔对比

*Past and Present of the Church
of Lubiąż Abbey*

　　从第二次世界大战前拍摄的黑白照片（第38页）中我们可以看到卢比昂日修道院的教堂内饰充满了巴洛克艺术的动感与激情，每个细节都精美异常。然而经过战争的无情洗礼后，虽然建筑的主体保留了下来，但内部的装饰则损毁得十分严重。而有幸留下来的部分，都收藏在各地的博物馆当中。

　　From the archived picture taken before World War II, the church of Lubiąż was fully decorated with the extremely exquisite Baroque elements, but in the picture of nowadays, because of the dreadful war only the main structure of the building itself left, and small parts of the sculptures are fortunately acquired by some local museums.

天使唱诗班座椅雕塑群

The Angelic Choir Stalls

　　马蒂亚斯·施坦因尔的大型雕塑作品，天使唱诗班座椅雕塑群创作于 1681—1696 年。安装在卢比昂日修道院教堂中殿的两侧，由 18 个座椅和 2 个木屋组成，座椅间用茛苕叶形装饰作为分割。在叶形装饰之间，站立着弹奏着各式乐器的小天使；在其上方的飞檐上，雕刻着或站或坐的大天使，南边的演奏弹拨乐器，北边的演奏管乐器。伴随修士的祷告天使唱诗班坐在这里唱赞歌，意在用音乐和歌唱赞美上帝。这组造型丰富的室内雕塑群证明了艺术家生动的想象力。

　　During 1681-1696, Matthias Steinl created the angelic choir stalls for the abbey church in Lubiąż, which decorated both sides of the central nave. It consisted of 18 seats and two loges separated with carved acanthus mollis leaves. In the leaves, there were figures of putti playing various instruments. Sculptures of standing or sitting angels playing on plucked string instruments (on the south side) and on wind instruments (on the north side) were located Above them, on the cornice. The idea of the stalls' decoration was to praise God with music and singing. The choir of angels accompanied the monks in their prayers and singing. The remarkable, rich ornamental forms from the angelic choir stalls proved the vivid imagination of the artist.

小天使
Putti

马蒂亚斯 · 施坦因尔（约 1644—1727）
1676—1696 年，天使唱诗班雕塑群，
卢比昂日修道院教堂，西里西亚
椴木，石膏，彩绘，鎏金

Steinl, Matthias (ca. 1644-1727)
1676-1696, angelic choir stalls, church
of Lubiąż Abbey, Silesia
Lime wood, gesso, polychromed,
gilded

吹号小天使（MNWr XII-1107）
高 51 厘米，宽 41 厘米，厚 21 厘米
Putto playing the Horn (MNWr XII-1107)
Height 51 cm, width 41 cm, depth 21 cm

吹喇叭小天使（MNWr XII-1110）
高 60.5 厘米，宽 32 厘米，厚 25.5 厘米
Putto playing the Cornett (MNWr XII-1110)
Height 60.5 cm, width 32 cm, depth 25.5 cm

演奏提琴小天使（MNWr XII-1091）
高 53 厘米，宽 32.5 厘米，厚 35 厘米
Putto playing the Violin (MNWr XII-1091)
Height 53 cm, width 32.5 cm, depth 35 cm

吹笛小天使（MNWr XII-1106）
高 66 厘米，宽 48 厘米，厚 24 厘米
Putto playing the Pipe (MNWr XII-1106)
Height 66 cm, width 48 cm, depth 24 cm

V

演奏叉铃小天使（MNWr XII-1090）
高 60 厘米，宽 43 厘米，厚 24 厘米
Putto playing the Sistrum (MNWr XII-1090)
Height 60 cm, width 43 cm, depth 24 cm

VI

演奏敲弦古钢琴小天使（MNWr XII-1105）
小天使：高 69 厘米，宽 51 厘米，厚 49 厘米
琴：高 60 厘米，宽 27 厘米，厚 8 厘米
Putto playing the Clavichord (MNWr XII-1105)
Putto: height 69 cm, width 51 cm, depth 49 cm
Clavichord: height 60 cm, width 27 cm, depth 8 cm

27

马蒂亚斯 · 施坦因尔（约 1644—1727）

坐狮与小天使

1675—1687 年，卢比昂日修道院，西里西亚
椴木，石膏，彩绘，鎏金
左：高 136 厘米，宽 59 厘米，厚 44 厘米
MNWr XII-1077
右：高 134 厘米，宽 60 厘米，厚 47.5 厘米
MNWr XII-1080

Steinl, Matthias (ca. 1644-1727)

Sitting Lion with a Putto

1675-1687, Lubiąż Abbey, Silesia
Lime wood, gesso, polychromed, gilded
Left: height 136 cm, width 59 cm, depth 44 cm
MNWr XII-1077
Right: height 134 cm, width 60 cm, depth 47.5 cm
MNWr XII-1080

（28）马蒂亚斯·施坦因尔（约 1644—1727）
三个天使头像装饰及莨苕叶形装饰

1672—1691 年，天使唱诗班座椅，卢比昂日修道院，西里西亚（左、右）
1675—1687 年，天使唱诗班座椅，卢比昂日修道院，西里西亚（中）
椴木，石膏，彩绘，鎏金
左：高 104 厘米；宽 30 厘米，厚 16 厘米，MNWr XII-493
右：高 104 厘米，宽 27 厘米，厚 20 厘米，MNWr XII-494
中：高 67.5 厘米，宽 118 厘米，厚 11 厘米，MNWr XII-1060

Steinl, Matthias（ca. 1644-1727）
Bracket with three angel's heads and acanthus leaves

1672-1691, angelic choir stalls, Lubiąż Abbey, Silesia（left and right）
1675-1687, angelic choir stalls, Lubiąż Abbey, Silesia（middle）
Lime wood, gesso, polychromed, gilded
Left: height 104 cm, width 30 cm, depth 16 cm, MNWr XII-493
Right: height 104 cm, width 27 cm, depth 20 cm. MNWr XII-494
Middle: height 67.5 cm, width 118 cm, depth 11 cm. MNWr XII-1060

 马蒂亚斯·施坦因尔（约1644—1727）

贝壳图案檐口装饰及莨苕叶形装饰

1675—1687年，天使唱诗班座椅，卢比昂日修道院，西里西亚
椴木，石膏，彩绘，鎏金
左：高136厘米，宽56.5厘米，厚34.5厘米，MNWr XII-1104
右：高117厘米，宽51厘米，厚36厘米，MNWr XII-1093
中：高91厘米，宽122厘米，厚12.5厘米，MNWr XII-1082

Steinl, Matthias (ca. 1644-1727)

Shell motif from the cornice and acanthus leaves

1675-1687, angelic choir stalls, Lubiąż Abbey, Silesia
Lime wood, gesso, polychromed, gilded
Left: Height 136 cm, width 56.5 cm, depth 34.5 cm, MNWr XII-1104
Right: Height 117 cm, width 51 cm, depth 36 cm, MNWr XII-1093
Middle: Height 91 cm, width 122 cm, depth 12.5 cm, MNWr XII-1082

30 马蒂亚斯·施坦因尔（约 1644—1727）

贝壳图案檐口装饰及莨苕叶形装饰

1675—1687 年，天使唱诗班座椅，卢比昂日修道院，西里西亚
椴木，石膏，彩绘，鎏金
左：高 137 厘米，宽 45 厘米，厚 27.5 厘米，MNWr XII-594
右：高 82 厘米，宽 59.5 厘米，厚 39 厘米，MNWr XII-1108
中：高 91 厘米，宽 134 厘米，厚 14 厘米，MNWr XII-1085

Steinl, Matthias (ca.1644-1727)

Shell motif from the cornice and acanthus leaves

1675-1687, angelic choir stalls, Lubiąż Abbey, Silesia
Lime wood, gesso, polychromed, gilded
Left: Height 137 cm, width 45 cm, depth 27.5 cm, MNWr XII-594
Right: Height 82 cm, width 59.5 cm, depth 39 cm, MNWr XII-1108
Middle: Height 91 cm, width 134 cm, depth 14 cm, MNWr XII-1085

小天使饰带一组

Friezes with Putti

马蒂亚斯·施坦因尔（约 1644—1727）

小天使饰带

约 1700 年，卢比昂日修道院，西里西亚
椴木，石膏，彩绘
58 厘米 × 90 厘米 × 10 厘米
MNWr XII–301

Steinl, Matthias (ca. 1644-1727)

Frieze with a Putto

ca. 1700, Lubiąż Abbey, Silesia
Lime wood, gesso, polychromed
58 cm × 90 cm × 10 cm
MNWr XII-301

马蒂亚斯·施坦因尔（约 1644—1727）

小天使饰带

约 1700 年，卢比昂日修道院，西里西亚
椴木，石膏，彩绘
58 厘米 × 90 厘米 × 10 厘米
MNWr XII–300

Steinl, Matthias (ca. 1644-1727)

Frieze with a Putto

ca. 1700, Lubiąż Abbey, Silesia
Lime wood, gesso, polychromed
58 cm × 90 cm × 10 cm
MNWr XII-300

马蒂亚斯 · 施坦因尔（约 1644—1727）

大卫

17 世纪 80 年代，卢比昂日修道院，西里西亚
木胎，石膏，泥，鎏金，彩绘
高 110 厘米，宽 86 厘米，厚 56 厘米
MNWr XII-559

Steinl, Matthias (ca. 1644-1727)
David

1680-1690, Lubiąż Abbey, Silesia
Wood with gesso, polychromed and gilded
on red and yellow bole
Height 110 cm, width 86 cm, depth 56 cm
MNWr XII-559

马蒂亚斯·施坦因尔（约 1644—1727）
先知

17 世纪 80 年代，卢比昂日修道院，西里西亚
木胎，石膏，泥，鎏金，彩绘
高 115 厘米，宽 45 厘米，厚 45 厘米
MNWr XII-558

Steinl, Matthias (ca. 1644-1727)
The Prophet

1680-1690, Lubiąż Abbey, Silesia
Wood with gesso, polychromed and
gilded on red and yellow bole
Height 115 cm, width 45 cm, depth 45 cm
MNWr XII-558

34

马蒂亚斯·施坦因尔（约 1644—1727）
大天使米迦勒

约 1700 年，卢比昂日修道院，西里西亚
木胎，石膏，泥，鎏金，彩绘
高 110 厘米，宽 86 厘米，厚 56 厘米
MNWr XII-1182

Steinl, Matthias (ca. 1644-1727)
Saint Michael the Archangel

ca. 1700, Lubiąż Abbey, Silesia
Wood with gesso, polychromed and gilded
on red and yellow bole
Height 110 cm, width 86 cm, depth 56 cm
MNWr XII-1182

第三单元
市民生活的重建

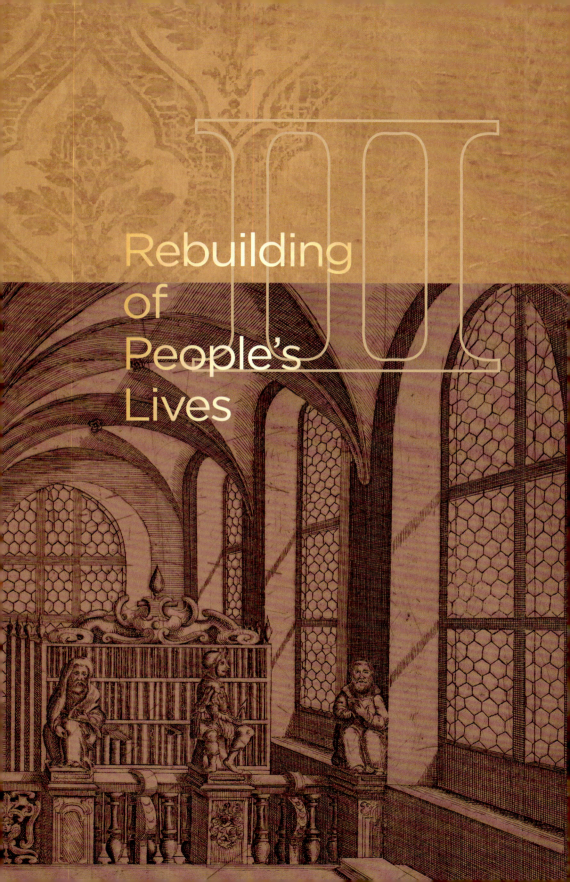

III

Rebuilding of People's Lives

　　1618 年至 1648 年的三十年战争，起因于宗教矛盾，继而演变成席卷整个欧洲的争霸之战，对整个德意志地区，包括西里西亚都造成了极其严重的破坏。伴随着战后西里西亚各个城市经济的复苏，城市中产在这一时期兴起，既有行会工匠、小企业主，也包括医生、政府公职人员等。随着经济地位的上升，他们成为能够左右城市发展的新兴市民阶层，也是巴洛克时代的典型人物——他们崇尚勤劳的工作，也追求富庶的生活；注重教育且善于思考。尽管深深体会到瘟疫、战争、自然与人为的灾难随时威胁着人们的生命，但他们依旧积极参与创造社会价值，享受着社会生活的美好，并期待着为他人所铭记。正如展览里呈现的这些巴洛克风格和样式的金属手工艺品，不仅展现了精湛的技艺和他们的财富，也是他们为这个世界留下的印记。

　　此外，这些酒杯、银器、迎客杯和武器等，都是西里西亚引以为傲的手工艺品代表，大量出口到东欧和西欧。手工匠人们因其过人的智慧和高超的技艺而受到赞誉，激发着他们丰富的创造力和想象力。这是一个巴洛克的世界——一个由人所创，为人所用的世界。

　　The Thirty Years War (1618-1648) fought between Catholics and Protestants was driven by religious tensions rooted deeply in the fragmented Holy Roman Empire. It gradually developed into a more general conflict involving most of the European great powers. It was one of the most destructive conflicts in the German speaking area including Silesia. The postwar economic recovery in Silesia provided opportunities for the arrival of the city burgher class. This group of people engaged in all kinds of social activities and skilled occupations. Craftsmen in trade guilds, owners of small businesses, doctors and, government officials were some fine examples. The rapid growth in wealth empowered this newly risen burgher class to play a crucial role in the Baroque era's city development. Hard working and well-to-do, the burgher class valued the importance of education and had active minds. Having realised that common people's lives could be threatened, at any given moment, by catastrophic events, such as plagues, wars, natural or man-made disasters, yet they did not cease performing their professional duties, adding values to society, or celebrating the joy of life, and was always longing to be well remembered. Just as the handicrafts are presented in the exhibition, which are items with excellent skills and showcases the riches and the footprints of people who produced or possessed them.

　　Silesia was also famous for the funerary shields, pewter tankards, silver vessels, welcome cups and elements of armaments. These handicrafts representing the local high-level applied arts, as they were exported to both western and eastern of Europe. The admiration was the driving power to encourage and inspire the artisans. This is a world created by man to fulfil all his needs — a Baroque world.

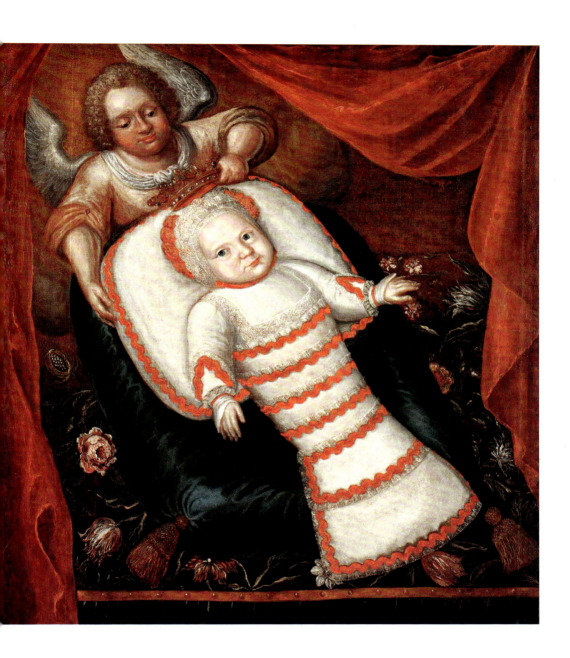

35

佚名画家
婴儿与守护天使

1650—1675 年
布面油画
90 厘米 × 80 厘米
MNWr VIII-620

Unknown artist
Infant with the Guardian Angel

Third quarter of the 17th century
Oil on canvas
90 cm × 80 cm
MNWr VIII-620

佚名艺术家
附盖罐

17 世纪末，西里西亚
银鎏金
高 17 厘米，直径 12 厘米
MNWr V–1847

Unknown artist
Can with lid

End of the 17th century, Silesia
Gilded silver
Height 17 cm, diameter 12 cm
MNWr V–1847

 小格特弗里德·福格尔
弥撒用器皿

1679 年，西里西亚
银
长 9.5 厘米，宽 8.3 厘米，高 4.5 厘米
MNWr V−1859

Vogel, Gottfried the Younger

Pyx

1679, Silesia
Silver
Length 9.5 cm, width 8.3 cm, height 4.5 cm
MNWr V−1859

盾形葬礼铭牌
Funerary Shield

16—20 世纪初，德语国家有一种葬俗：行会或出师学徒兄弟会在葬礼上为亡故成员的棺材上悬挂盾形铭牌。当时的西里西亚属于德语地区，因此也遵循这类葬俗。在西里西亚的弗罗茨瓦夫市至今共发现了166 块典型的葬礼铭牌，可见这一传统曾经格外流行。最初的铭牌是由丝绸、天鹅绒、亚麻等纺织品制成的，随后铜和黄铜等质地的更为常见，17 世纪中叶出现了银制铭牌。由于铭牌是由行会订制的，因此上面常刻有行会标志，有时也刻有宗教图案。每件铭牌都制作得十分精美，说明了人们对逝者的怀念和对葬礼的重视。

A custom of hanging shields on the coffin during the funeral services of deceased members of guilds and fraternities of journeymen was practiced in German countries from the 16th through the early 20th century. This tradition was exceptionally eagerly cultivated in Wrocław: as many as 166 specimens are known to have survived. Funerary shields were initially made from fabrics: silk, especially silk velvet, cloth, and linen. Textile shields were later replaced by those made of copper or brass. Silver shields appeared in the mid-17th century. The funerary shield usually featured the guild's emblem set in a decorative, elaborate frame and sometimes also religious motifs.

38

雅各布·黑德尔霍福尔（活跃于 1664—1690 年）
弗罗茨瓦夫剪毛呢工行会葬礼铭牌

1665 年，弗罗茨瓦夫，西里西亚
银鎏金
47 厘米 × 39 厘米
MNWr V-1880

Hedelhofer, Jacob (fl. 1664-1690)

*Funerary shield of the guild of cloth
shearers from Wrocław*

1665, Wrocław, Silesia
Gilded silver
47 cm × 39 cm
MNWr V-1880

汉斯·施佩特（1608—1659）
弗罗茨瓦夫新城布商出师学徒兄弟会葬礼铭牌

1656 年，弗罗茨瓦夫，西里西亚
银鎏金
43.1 厘米 × 35.7 厘米
MNWr V–1876

Späth, Hans (1608-1659)

Funerary shield of the fraternity of journeymen cloth shearers in the New Town in Wrocław

1656, Wrocław, Silesia
Gilded silver
43.1 cm × 35.7 cm
MNWr V-1876

佚名艺术家
弗罗茨瓦夫渔夫行会葬礼铭牌

1675 年，弗罗茨瓦夫，西里西亚
黄铜鎏金
47 厘米 × 45 厘米
MNWr V-1876

Unknown artist
Funerary shield of guild of fishermen in Wrocław

1675, Wrocław, Silesia
Gilded brass
47 cm × 45 cm
MNWr V-1876

佚名艺术家
拉齐布日钉工及铁匠行会葬礼铭牌

1683 年，拉齐布日，西里西亚
红铜鎏金
37.5 厘米 × 32.8 厘米
MNWr V-2263

Unknown artist

Funerary shield of the guild of nailers and blacksmiths in Racibórz

1683, Racibórz, Silesia
Gilded copper
37.5 cm × 32.8 cm
MNWr V-2263

汉斯 · 博伊 (1615—1671)

弗罗茨瓦夫制革行会葬礼铭牌

1658 年，弗罗茨瓦夫，西里西亚
银鎏金
直径 45.8 厘米
MNWr XV-244

Boy, Hans (1615-1671)

Funerary shield of the guild of whittawers and chamois-leather makers in Wrocław

1658, Wrocław, Silesia
Gilded silver
Diameter 45.8 cm
MNWr XV-244

43

叶赫米亚斯·比德尔曼
弗罗茨瓦夫姜饼生产者行会啤酒杯

1667 年，西里西亚
铅锡合金
高 19 厘米，宽 18 厘米
MNWr V-269

Biederman, Jeremias
Tankard of the guild of gingerbread makers from Wrocław

1667, Silesia
Pewter
Height 19 cm, width 18 cm
MNWr V-269

汉斯 · 莱恩
弗罗茨瓦夫屠夫行会锡壶

1665 年，弗罗茨瓦夫，西里西亚
铅锡合金
高 58 厘米，宽 30 厘米
MNWr V–273

Lein, Hans
Jug of the guild of butchers in Wrocław

1665, Wrocław, Silesia
Pewter
Height 58 cm, width 30 cm
MNWr V–273

汉斯·科贝尔
弗罗茨瓦夫屠夫行会杯子

银
左：1660 年，弗罗茨瓦夫，西里西亚
高 9.7 厘米，口径 7.3 厘米
MNWr V-645
右：1663 年，弗罗茨瓦夫，西里西亚
高 9.5 厘米，口径 7.6 厘米
MNWr V-650

Körber, Hans

Cups of the guild of butchers in Wrocław

Silver
Left: 1660, Wrocław, Silesia
Height 9.7 cm, diameter 7.3 cm
MNWr V-645
Right: 1663, Wrocław, Silesia
Height 9.5 cm, diameter 7.6 cm
MNWr V-650

46

克里斯托弗 · 汉斯
克沃兹科染料行会酒壶

1659 年，西里西亚
锤揲和加工的黄铜及红铜
高 44.5 厘米，最大宽度 28 厘米
MNWr V-1838

Christoph, Hans
Pitcher of the dyers' guild of Kłodzko

1659, Silesia
Repoussé and wrought brass and copper
Height 44.5 cm, max. width 28 cm
MNWr V-1838

迎客杯
Wilkom

迎客杯一词来自德语 Willkommen，是一种大容积、刻有装饰图案的红酒或啤酒杯，一般用于行会庆典。比如，刚刚出师的学徒入会典礼或宴请其他行会的嘉宾，大家要将杯中的酒一饮而尽，以示欢迎。有时所有宾客围坐一桌，轮流饮用一杯酒。这种杯身巨大、装饰华美的酒杯彰显了行会的富足和声望。

Wilkom (from German: Willkommen - greeting; the cup of welcome) or Welcome cup is a big, decorative cup used for drinking wine or beer during guild ceremonies. The journeymen who just completed an apprenticeship and guests from other guilds had to drink from it to the bottom as a form of greeting. Sometimes a wilkom was used by all the feasters and circulated around the table. The grandness and beauty of the guild's wilkom demonstrated its wealth and prestige.

莱茵霍尔德·克里斯托弗·蒂特耶
附盖迎客杯

1661 年，希维德尼察
铅锡合金
高 53 厘米，最大宽度 14 厘米
MNWr V–593

Tietje, Reinhold Christoph
Wilkom with a lid

1661, Świdnica
Pewter
Height 53 cm, max. width 14 cm
MNWr V-593

48

佚名艺术家
亚沃尔制桶工行会迎客杯

1668 年，亚沃尔，西里西亚
铅锡合金
高 39 厘米，最大宽度 15 厘米
MNWr V-431

Unknown artist
Wilkom of the guild of coopers from Jawor

1668, Silesia
Pewter
Height 39 cm, max. width 15 cm
MNWr V-431

49

梅尔基奥尔·博特
希维德尼察石匠砖匠行会迎客杯

1688 年，希维德尼察，西里西亚
铅锡合金
高 45.5 厘米，最大宽度 18 厘米
MNWr V–555

Bothe, Melchior

*Wilkom of the guild of
stonemasons and bricklayers
from Świdnica*

1688, Świdnica, Silesia
Pewter
Height 45.5 cm, max. width 18 cm
MNWr V–555

迎客杯盾形吊饰
Pendant Shields of Wilkom

　　悬挂在迎客杯上的盾形吊饰是一种还愿进献之物。常由即将成为行会工匠师的出师学徒进献，或者其他人进献。这些人也可能不是该行会会员，时常是为了对行会的帮助表示感谢。

　　Pendant shields attached to a Wilkom were votive offerings, usually presented by former journeymen upon becoming guild masters and also by other donors, not necessarily the members of the guild, for various reasons, often to express gratitude for the guild's help.

佚名艺术家
**弗罗茨瓦夫木匠和磨坊主行会
迎客杯上的吊饰**

1677 年，弗罗茨瓦夫，西里西亚
银
10 厘米 × 8.5 厘米 × 1 厘米
MNWr V-2269

Unknown artist
Pendant shield of wilkom of the carpenters' and millers' guild in Wrocław

1677, Wrocław, Silesia
Silver
10 cm × 8.5 cm × 1 cm
MNWr V-2269

约翰·奥勒（1662—1698）
弗罗茨瓦夫篮子制作者行会迎客杯上的吊饰

1679 年，弗罗茨瓦夫，西里西亚
银
10 厘米 × 8 厘米 × 0.3 厘米
MNWr V-2466

Ohle, Johann (1662-1698)

*Pendant shield of wilkom of the basket makers'
guild in Wrocław*

1679, Wrocław, Silesia
Silver
10 cm × 8 cm × 0.3 cm
MNWr V-2466

52 佚名工匠
破甲剑

1658 年，中欧
钢、黄铜
长 131.5 厘米，宽 30 厘米，厚 7.5 厘米
MNWr IX-876

Unknown craftsman
Koncerz

1658, Central Europe
Steel, brass
Length 131.5 cm, width 30 cm,
depth 7.5 cm
MNWr IX-876

53 佚名工匠
破甲剑

约 1650 年，中欧
钢、黄铜
长 125.5 厘米，宽 21.5 厘米，厚 6.5 厘米
MNWr IX-924

Unknown craftsman
Koncerz

ca. 1650, Central Europe
Steel, brass
Length 125.5 cm, width 21.5 cm,
depth 6.5 cm
MNWr IX-924

佚名艺术家
带子弹袋的火药罐（切申风格）

约 1650 年，切申，西里西亚
木、铁、牛骨、珠母贝、皮革
长 14 厘米，宽 12 厘米，厚 6.5 厘米
MNWr IX–1525

Unknown artist (from Cieszyn School)
Powder flask with a bullet bag

ca. 1650, Cieszyn, Silesia
Wood, iron, ox bone, nacre and suede
Length 14 cm, width 12 cm, depth 6.5 cm
MNWr IX–1525

　　斧枪是一种可配套火药罐使用的火枪，它在枪口处装有一把斧子，因此还可以用于近身攻击。不过由于西里西亚特产的这种枪装饰过于华丽，其功能主要用于贵族狩猎和仪式。

　　The axe-pistol is a two-purpose weapon that can be used as a fire gun with the powder flask, and a hand weapon in direct combat with the axe blade. However, with its sophisticated form, it was preferably used in ceremonials or occasional bird hunting for the richest.

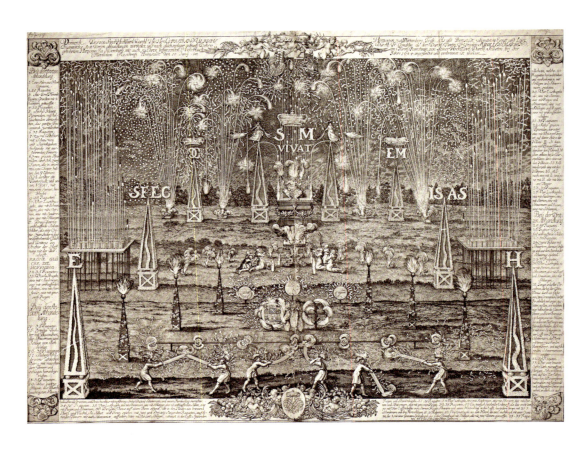

55

约翰 · 戈特弗里德 · 巴尔奇
别鲁图夫城堡前的烟花表演

1684 年，西里西亚
纸本铜版雕刻及蚀刻
68.2 厘米 × 89.9 厘米
MNWr VII-5027

Bartsch, Johann Gottfried
Festive Fireworks Display in Front of the Castle in Bierutów

1684, Silesia
Chalcography and with etching on paper
68.2 cm × 89.9 cm
MNWr VII-5027

56

格雷戈尔·比贝尔（1603—1659）
彼得·特鲁舍尔（约 1620—1667 年间颇具盛名）
1649 年部分垮塌的弗罗茨瓦夫圣伊丽莎白教堂

晚于 1649 年制版，约 1950 年印制，弗罗茨瓦夫，西里西亚
纸本铜版雕刻
61.4 厘米 × 48.6 厘米
MNWr VII-1129

Troschel, Peter (1603-1659);
Bieber,Gregor (fl ca. 1620-1667)
St. Elizabeth Church in Wrocław structure's partial collapse in 1649

After 1649 (print ca. 1950), Wrocław, Silesia
Chalcography on paper
61.4 cm × 48.6 cm
MNWr VII-1129

雅克布 · 林德尼兹

从南侧看弗罗茨瓦夫全景 △

1667 年制版，1883 年印制，弗罗茨瓦夫，西里西亚
纸本铜版雕刻
34.2 厘米 × 109.2 厘米
MNWr VII–1158

Lindnitz, Jacob

Panorama of Wrocław from the south

1667 (print from 1883), Wrocław, Silesia
Chalcography on paper
34.2 cm × 109.2 cm
MNWr VII- 1158

约翰 · 厄特尔 (1659—1726)
约翰 · 雅克布 · 爱博尔维塞，乔治 · 弗里德里希 · 提尔克

波普维兹高地附近奥得河的游船 ▷

1706 年，西里西亚
纸本铜版雕刻及蚀刻
40.3 厘米 × 54.4 厘米
MNWr VII–884

Oertel, Johann (1659-1726);
Eybelwieser , Johann Jacob;
Thielk, Georg Friedrich

Pleasure Boat on the Oder at the height of Popowice

1706, Silesia
Chalcography with etching on paper
40.3 cm × 54.4 cm
MNWr VII-884

Palm 122.

v Thum 23 Niclas Thor. 25 Fleischhaus 27 Orthig den Lust Fewern 29 Maberstein. 31 Vorstuck vorm Schw. Thor.
veinische Thor 24 Plawische thor 26 Schiesshewsen 28 Orth zu grossen Ragrasen 30 Pferd. und ander viehmarcet. 32 Mause Teich

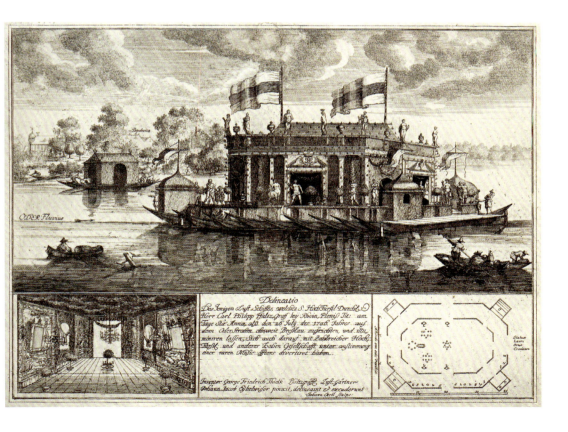

Prudnicz

ODER Fluvius

Delineatio
Der Jenigen Lust Schiffes, welches S. Hoch Fürstl Durchl.
Herr Carl Philipp Pfaltz Graff bey Rhein, Plenip Tit: am
Tage Ste Annæ, alß den 26 July der 1706 Jahres auff
dem Oder Stram, ohnweit Broslau, ausrichten, und itzo
miniren lassen, Sich auch darauf mit zahlreicher Hoch
Fürstl. und anderer hohen Gesellschafft unter anstimmung
einer raren Music öffters divertiret haben.

Inventor George Friedrich Thielk, Haltzgräff, Lust Gärtner
Johann Jacob Scheiweser pinxit, delineavit et excuderunt
Johann Carl sculps.

77

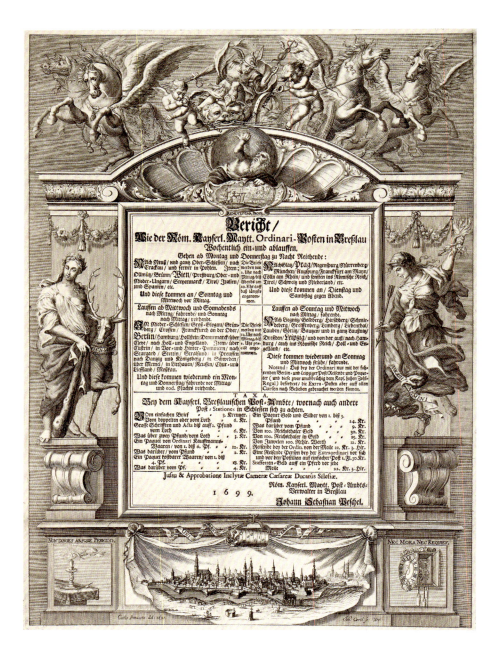

約翰·厄特尔 (1659—1726)
卡尔·普罗伊斯特
绘有弗罗茨瓦夫全景画的邮车时间表和价目表

1695—1699 年，弗罗茨瓦夫，西里西亚
纸本和纸板铜版雕刻
60.2 厘米 × 43.5 厘米
MNWr VII-6082

Oertel, Johann (1659-1726)
Preouste, Carl
Timetable and price list of postal services with panorama of Wrocław

1695-1699, Wrocław, Silesia
Chalcography on paper on cardboard
60.2 cm × 43.5 cm
MNWr VII-6082

59

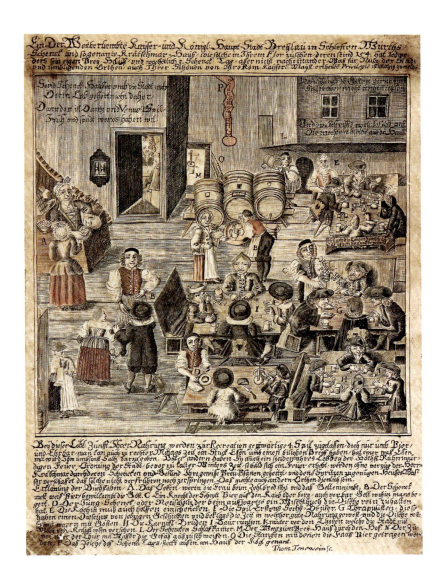

托马斯 · 耶尼维恩

奥瓦斯卡大街的客栈内景

60

早于 1717 年，西里西亚
彩色纸本铜版雕刻
28.6 厘米 × 21.2 厘米
MNWr VII-12388

61 约翰·切尔宁 (1650—1732)
从南侧看弗罗茨瓦夫全景

1679 年，弗罗茨瓦夫，西里西亚
纸本铜版雕刻
26.7 厘米 × 33.7 厘米
MNWr VII-1126

Tscherning, Johann (1650-1732)
Panorama of Wrocław from the south

1679, Wrocław, Silesia
Chalcography on paper
26.7 cm × 33.7 cm
MNWr VII-1126

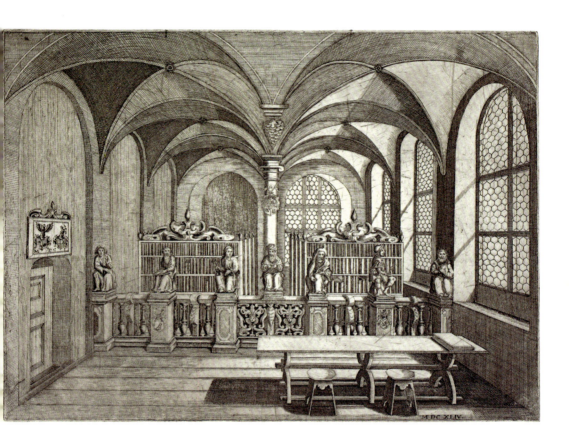

62 大卫 · 切尔宁（约 1615—1691）
圣抹大拉玛利亚教堂图书馆

1644 年，弗罗茨瓦夫，西里西亚
纸本铜版雕刻
22.6 厘米 × 30.2 厘米
MNWr VII–875/16

Tscherning, David (ca. 1615-1691)
Library at the St. Mary Magdalene Church in Wrocław

1644, Wrocław, Silesia
Chalcography on paper
22.6 cm × 30.2 cm
MNWr VII-875/16

结语

　　西里西亚的巴洛克时期是痛苦与美妙并存的时代，残酷的战争带来了伤痛，但艺术用它独特的魅力抚慰着在痛苦中挣扎的人们。艺术家们对创造性的追求，不断地感染着人们，并为他们带来令人向往的美，激励着人民走向重生。人们从未停止思考在短暂的人生中如何留下属于他们自己的印记。当我们跳出西里西亚这一域，俯瞰整个巴洛克时期的欧洲大地，战争还在继续，但社会进步的脚步也在继续，欧洲近代新的国际关系格局正在这个时代，以这样的方式，悄悄拉开了帷幕。

Epilogue

　　The Baroque period of Silesia was a time filled with beauty and yet pain. The pursuit of beliefs and eternity was not restrained by struggles and contradictory in ideology. A yearning for art and aesthetics mingled with heartbreaking suffering from wars. The admiringly enjoyable feelings brought about beautiful things and objects created for artistic purposes inspired artists; meanwhile artists' creativity which sparkled with passion and enthusiasm was appealing dearly to the public. What legacies one could leave to the world is always a proposition for many of us. Once we move our eyes away from the area of Silesia to view the continent of Europe as a whole, to no one's surprise, throughout history wars and conflicts have never been obstacles for social progress. New patterns of international relations in modern Europe could be forming quietly before they are even noticed.

展品文物说明
Descriptions of Exhibits

1. 沃尔夫冈·沙施密特肖像
Portrait of Wolfgang Scharschmidt

沃尔夫冈·沙施密特是弗罗茨瓦夫一位富裕的受过良好教育的律师和发明家。他与妻子一起继承了弗罗茨瓦夫市劳伦提乌斯·舒尔茨的一座16世纪庄园的一部分，这座庄园以其种植的众多奇花异草、收藏的艺术品和奇珍异宝而闻名。沙施密特在庄园里安装了各种会忽然喷水的装置，博参观者一笑。这些奇思妙想引得人们争相拜访，表明了巴洛克时代人们的猎奇心态。

更有趣的是这幅画作背后附有一个时钟装置，人物的眼珠可以左右移动，好像他的目光可以追随着观者一样。这个有趣的想法极具巴洛克特色，有可能是沙施密特自己的设计。

Wolfgang Scharschmidt was an affluent and well-educated lawyer and inventor. Together with his wife, they inherited part of Laurentius Scholz's 16th-century garden in Wrocław, which famous for its exotic plants and artworks, also the Scholz's cabinet of curiosities. In the garden, Scharschmidt installed different hydraulic machines of his invention that amused visitors by unexpectedly spilling water.

The portrait has a box attached to the back of the picture containing a clock mechanism that makes the pupils of the portrayed man move as if his gaze followed the viewer. This amusing concept is probably designed by Scharshmidt with typical Baroque style.

2. 阿诺德·费赖贝格尔肖像
Portrait of Arnold Freiberger

阿诺德·费赖贝格尔（1589—1672），是西多会的卢比昂日修道院院长，是第一位欣赏威尔曼才能的赞助人。这幅画是有记载最早的威尔曼的肖像画。人物面部和姿态略显僵硬，说明了这幅画是在费赖贝格尔本人去世后，威尔曼凭着记忆创作的，用于与其他已故修道院院长的画像一起悬挂在教堂的回廊里，想法来源于许多贵族住宅的祖先肖像画廊。费赖贝格尔的画像在威尔曼所有赞助人中是最多的。此外，画家也常隐秘地在其他作品中画入弗赖贝格尔的形象。

Abbot Arnold Freiberger (1589-1672) of the Cistercian abbey at Lubiąż was the first patron who fully appreciated Willmann's talent. These featured painting is the earliest known portrait painted by Willmann. The specific stiffness of the portrayed man's countenance and poise suggests that the painting could be created from memory, after Freiberger's death to be included in the portrait gallery of abbots in the church's ambulatory. This portrait gallery could corresponded to the galleries of ancestral portraits featured in many aristocratic residences. Among Willmann's patrons, Freiberger was one of the most frequently portrayed. Moreover, the artist often included his crypto-portraits in his other works.

3. 伯纳德·罗萨肖像
Portrait of Bernard Rosa

伯纳德·罗萨（1624—1696），是西多会的克热舒夫修道院院长，画家威尔曼的代理人之一。画中略显潦草的笔触透露出这幅画是为创作另一幅肖像画而画的草稿。尽管如此，威尔曼仍将此画保存在他的工作室中作为参照，以便在其他作品中创作罗萨的形象。这幅肖像对人物进行了深刻的心理分析，描绘了一位精力充沛、博学多才、新一代西里西亚天主教会修道院院长的形象。有趣的是，这幅画像的画布是从另一幅戴珍珠的女人画像上裁剪下来的，画家用它再次创作了这幅肖像。

Abbot Bernard Rosa (1624-1696) of the Cistercian abbey at Krzeszów, was one of Willmann's most important patrons. The sketchy, manner of its execution indicates that this is a painting study for a "proper" portrait. Nevertheless, the artist kept it in his workshop and used as a reference for other works commissioned by Rosa. It steps out with a profound psychological analysis of the model —energetic and savant representative of the new generation of the Silesian Catholic Church. Interestingly, this image was painted on a piece of recycled canvas cut from another painting (depicting a woman wearing pearls).

4、5. 汉斯·恩斯特·瓦恩斯多夫和 安娜·索菲·瓦恩斯多夫肖像

4. *Portrait of Hans Ernst Warnsdorf*
5. *Portrait of Anna Sophie Warnsdorf*

　　这两件巨幅肖像描绘了巴洛克时期西里西亚贵族汉斯·恩斯特和他的妻子安娜·索菲。作为身份的象征，瓦恩斯多夫夫妇二人的服饰反映了17世纪中期欧洲的宫廷风尚。尽管画作中人物姿态略显僵硬，但是画作中反映的内容仍然很精确，具有独特的魅力。从这个意义上说，这两幅肖像具有很重要的作用。这对夫妇衣服的颜色和纹理十分协调，用来强调婚姻的和谐美满。其中，汉斯·恩斯特华贵时尚的奶白色金色锦缎上衣点缀着钻石钮扣，夸张的灯笼袖配上黑色缎带和金色首饰，手中拿着装饰有花式围钻和红绿色长羽毛的宽檐黑色帽子，莱茵格雷夫型朱红色马裤镶有银色花边。他还穿着带马刺靴子佩戴着长剑，表明了他骑兵尉官的身份。他的妻子以一种高贵的方式凸显出她高腰厚褶的裙子。她身着昂贵的奶白色和金色锦缎长礼服，搭配红色蝴蝶结图案和白色蕾丝领，配套的小巧手套、珍珠和玛瑙珠宝首饰与礼服相得益彰。精致的手套是地位的证明，即使不戴上也要显示出来。她的发型前部竖直，两耳处对称，后部则梳成发髻，另外，亮出前额带有卷发的发型在当时十分流行。她左手中的柠檬象征着生命和忠诚的爱情。这两幅画左上角和右上角分别有一首短诗是关于贵族夫妇的。汉斯·恩斯特的那首专他虔诚而谦卑，与他传说中的暴躁脾气似乎并不相符。他妻子的那首诗描述着一种向往正直生活和远离邪恶的承诺。

These two monumental portraits depict a noble couple from Silesia in the Baroque era. The portraits speak the volumes the importance of the dress as the symbol of statues and reflect the courtly fashion of the mid-17th century within great precision and considerable charm, though it was painted with a certain stiffness of attitudes and gestures. The colours and fabrics of the couple's dress are coordinated: this was a way to emphasise marital harmony. The fashionable dress of Hans Ernst Warnsdorf, a Silesian nobleman and cavalry officer, combines refine adornments - cream and gold brocade pour point with diamond buttons, fancy pinned up wide shirt's sleeves with black ribbons, gold jewelry, large black hat with aigrette, diamond rosette and long red-and-green plume, Rhingrave-type vermilion trousers without lace or ribbons but with silver edging - with military accessories: boots with spurs and rapier, suitable for his cavalry warrant officer range. A poem in the top left corner - pious and full of humbleness - is contrary to his alleged violent temper. Anna Sophie Warsndorf was married to Hans Ernst. She displays the raised-waistline dress with its heavy folded skirt in a majestic and dignified manner. Her rich gown made of cream and gold damask with red bows and white lace collar is complemented with small matching gloves, pearls and onyx pieces of jewelry. Elegant gloves were a status accessory, included even if not put on. The fashionable hairdo with spiral curls and exposed forehead. The hair is parted horizontally in front and also symmetrically above the ears, and in the back, it is arranged in a bun. Lemon in her left hand symbolises life and faithful love. A poem in the top right corner is a promise to lead a virtuous life and keep away from evil.

6. 汉斯·恩斯特肖像

Portrait of Hans Ernst von Langenau

　　作品中描绘的是年轻的西里西亚贵族汉斯·恩斯特·冯·兰格瑙，他死于"九年战争"，即对抗法国路易十四的大同盟战争期间（1688—1697）。在这幅遗像中他的形象出现了两次，除了画面中间外，在左下角，他还出现在一群倒下的士兵中，同样身着独特的黄色紧身长袍（一种源于军队的外衣）和黑色胸甲。

Hans Ernst von Langenau, a young Silesian nobleman, was killed during the Nine Years War (1688-1697). The artist depicted him twice in this featured portrait. In addition to the principal portrait, he is also represented, dressed in the same distinctive yellow justacorps (fashionable coat of military origins) and black cuirass, in the bottom left corner, among the warriors fallen in the battle.

7. 斐迪南三世皇帝停灵室

Castrum Doloris of Emperor Ferdinand III

停灵室（来自拉丁语"悲伤城堡"）是一个专有名称，用于形容搭建或遮盖在灵柩或棺椁外的建筑结构和装饰，以体现逝者的威望或崇高地位。版画中的停灵室由梅尔基奥·斐迪南·加斯金在弗罗茨瓦夫的圣马蒂亚斯教堂设计建造，以哀悼神圣罗马帝国皇帝斐迪南三世（1608—1657）。放置逝者遗体的灵柩台被烛光环绕，四个卷曲的柱子撑起方尖碑形状的鲜丽锦缎华盖遮盖上方，华盖上装饰着皇帝的徽章和圣母玛丽亚的画像。灵柩台周围的四个方尖碑顶部装饰着皇冠，并刻有符号和铭文，颂扬逝者的美德。灵柩台左边的雕塑代表着正义，右边雕塑是虔诚的化身。

The Latin term castrum doloris (literally "castle of grief") is a name for the structure and decorations sheltering or accompanying the catafalque or bier that signify the prestige or high estate of the deceased.

The print depicts the castrum doloris erected by Melchior Ferdinand de Gaschin in St Matthias' Church in Wrocław to honour the Emperor Ferdinand III (1608-1657). The catafalque is surrounded by candles, the canopy above it is shaped into an obelisk supported on four twisted columns. The obelisk is decorated with the emperor's emblems and topped by with the statue of Madonna Immaculata. Around the catafalque, there are four obelisks with sculls wearing imperial crowns, decorated with symbols and inscriptions glorifying the virtues of the deceased. The catafalque is flanked by the personifications of Justice (left) and Piety (right).

8. 利奥波德一世皇帝墓志铭

Epitaph of Leopold the Great

利奥波德一世（1640—1705）是哈布斯堡王朝时期神圣罗马帝国的皇帝、匈牙利、克罗地亚、波西米亚国王，斐迪南三世次子。因其在对抗奥斯曼土耳其帝国的战争中大获全胜而一战成名。这场战争结束于1699年，大大削弱了奥斯曼帝国在中东欧地区的势力。这幅版画中展示了利奥波德一世葬礼的场景。他遗体躺在鲜丽的锦缎遮盖的灵柩里，烛光照亮四周。画面下方，一只鹰紧握的涡卷饰牌上，印有一首赞美逝者伟大的诗篇。

Leopold I Habsburg(1640-1705), the Holy Roman Emperor, King of Hungary, Croatia, and Bohemia, is remembered mostly for his victory over the Ottoman Empire following a long war that ended in 1699. The war significantly diminished Turkish influence in east-central Europe. The print shows him lying in state on a canopied catafalque, surrounded by lit candles. The decorative cartouche held by an eagle is inscribed with a poem glorifying the deceased monarch and his deeds.

9. 弗罗茨瓦夫医生菲利普·雅克布·萨赫斯·勒文海姆肖像

Portrait of doctor Philipp Jacob Sachs a Löwenheim

10. 弗罗茨瓦夫议员库伯福尔伯格的西吉斯蒙德侯爵肖像

Portrait of councilman Sigismund Fürst von Kupferberg

11. 议员及司库约翰尼斯·哥兹肖像

Portrait of councilman and treasurer Johannes Gotz

12. 弗罗茨瓦夫议员大卫·冯·伊比恩·史特拉西维兹肖像

Portrait of Wrocław councilman David von Eben auf Strachwitz

13. 弗罗茨瓦夫议员约翰·西吉斯蒙德·豪纳尔德肖像

Portrait of Wrocław councilman Johann Sigismund Haunold

14. 牧师约翰尼斯·阿库鲁图斯肖像

Portrait of pastor Johannes Akolut

15. 牧师米夏埃尔·海尔曼肖像

Portrait of pastor Michael Hermann

16. 男爵西吉斯蒙德·海因里希肖像

Portrait of baron Sigismund Heinrich von Biebran

17. 希维德尼察公国的贵族沙夫高士伯爵克里斯托弗·利奥波德肖像

Portrait of starost of Świdnica Duchy, Christophor Leopold count von Schafgotsch

18. 自画像

Self- portrait

这是一幅画家的自画像。画家所描绘的自己身着休闲装，姿态放松，平凡、发福的面貌显然并不是理想化的气息。然而，他凝望的眼神却焕发出了自信的光芒和巴洛克时代典型的艺术自主性。威尔曼创作这幅作品，很可能是因为他希望入选《德国建筑雕塑与绘画艺术学院》（1683）一书。由于佛罗伦萨版画家斯特凡诺·德拉·贝拉（1610—1664）曾入选此书的前一版本，因此威尔曼借鉴了他的肖像作品。威尔曼希望可以像其他著名的艺术家一样，凭借该书而青史留名。

Artist depicted himself in a casual outfit and pose, though his ordinary and portly face is not idealised. However, his gaze expresses self-confidence and artistic independence typical for the Baroque era. This portrait was made probably in connection with Willmann's efforts to be included in Teutsche Academie (or German Academy of the Noble Arts of Architecture, Sculpture and Painting, 1683), a prestigious art dictionary with biographies of the greatest artists. The image is based on the portrait of Florence printmaker Stefano della Bella (1610-1664) published in the previous edition of Teutsche Academie. It seems that Willmann wanted to look like other famous artists honoured in the publication.

19. 俄耳甫斯为动物演奏音乐

Orpheus playing music for the animals

在希腊神话里，俄耳甫斯是阿波罗和缪斯女神卡利俄佩之子，也是一位才华横溢的诗人、歌手和七弦琴演奏家。他演奏的神奇音乐可以给人乃至神灵带去快乐，甚至能够让野兽俯首帖耳。这幅画描绘了年轻的俄耳甫斯坐在岩石上弹奏琴的情景。他身着古典时代装束，头戴月桂花环（象征永恒的名望），画面中聚集在他的周围的有鹿、狗、猴子、豹子、野兔、火鸡、孔雀和喜鹊等动物，它们都侧耳倾听。画家展示了音乐的普世作用，即所有生物都能受到艺术的感染。黑暗、茂密的森林和画幅左边留白处照来的光线营造了一种温馨而神秘的氛围。

Orpheus, in Greek mythology son of Apollo and muse Kaliope. He was a brilliant poet, singer and lyre player. Thanks to his miraculous music he could charm people and gods and even tame wild beasts. The painting depicts young Orpheus sitting on a rock in the Classical fashion and laurel wreath (symbol of eternal fame) on his head, playing harp, surrounded by listening wilds and domestic animals: a deer, a dog, a monkey, a leopard, hares, a turkey, peacocks and magpies to represent all the continents known at that time. In this way, Willmann showed the universal role of music as the art accessible to all creatures. Dark, dense forest and light coming from the clearance on the left gives the scene an intimate and mysterious atmosphere.

20. 绑架珀尔塞福涅

The Abduction of Persephone

珀尔塞福涅是古希腊神话中冥界的王后，她是众神之王宙斯和农业女神得墨忒尔的女儿，被冥王哈迪斯绑架到冥界与其结婚，成为冥后。得墨忒尔到处寻找她的女儿，后来在宙斯调解下，珀尔塞福涅每年的一大半时间与母亲生活，冬天则和哈迪斯一起度过。每个冬天，大地都会因此而荒芜。画面中，珀尔塞福涅与她的同伴一起摘花，随后被哈迪斯绑架，哈迪斯的战车在土地上留下一道道裂痕。威尔曼借鉴了约瑟夫·海因茨同主题画作的构图（德累斯顿历代大师画廊藏，约1595年绘），但独创的色彩和光线布局，让中央场景更具活力，并在战车周围添加了一片红云代替了海因茨画作中的田园风光。

In Greek mythology Persephone (Kore) was the daughter of Zeus and Demeter. She abducted by Hades, the divine ruler of the underworld, who made her his wife. Demeter searched for her daughter everywhere. Zeus decided that Persephone would be spending more than a half year with her mother and winter months with Hades. Her cyclical disappearance would leave earth barren for winter. The painting shows Persephone picking up flowers with her companions and about to be abducted by Hades, whose chariot burst through a crack in the ground. Willmann repeated the composition after Joseph Heintz painting (ca. 1595 - Gemäldegalerie Alte Meister in Dresden) but created his arrangement of colour and light, made the central scene more dynamic, and added a red cloud around the chariot that replaced the idyllic landscape of Heintz's work.

21. 逃往埃及
The Flight into Egypt

这幅画的题材取自《圣经》，画面描绘了为躲避希律王的杀戮，耶稣全家逃往埃及的场景。画中的景观具有鲜明特点，在威尔曼的其他作品中也有类似特征：不对称分割的场景和树形轮廓、拉低的地平线、右侧的悬崖、高饱和度且对比鲜明的色彩以及用硬笔沿对角排线表现天空。画面中周围的环境虽然让人感到危险逐渐逼近，人物显得的十分渺小而脆弱，但圣母玛利亚和义父约瑟面目表情十分的平静而温柔，专注于小耶稣，充满了抒情的氛围。

The theme of this painting is from the Bible, which depicts Joseph fled to Egypt with Mary and the infant Jesus since King Herod would seek the child to kill him. This landscape has many features present in other works by Willmann: the scene asymmetrically divided by a tree, the lowered horizon, the characteristic steep slope on the right, the saturated and contrasting colours, and the sky rendered by diagonal hatching executed with a stiff brush. In this disturbing, almost hostile setting, the Holy Family seems small, easy to overlook, but the group's expression is tender and lyrical.

22. 召唤圣马太
The Calling of St. Matthew

圣马太，又译为圣马窦，为基督12使徒之一。画面中描绘了他被基督召唤并成为使徒的场景。作品中对自然景观的深入描绘给人留下深刻的印象，以风景表现一幅叙事性的历史画卷，让画作左边出现的圣经场景不那么显眼，使整个作品看起来似乎像一幅含义简单的风景画。这幅画曾和现已遗失的《风景与隐士》一同挂在卢比昂日修道院的一个房间里。该画作的高超绘画技巧无疑证明了是威尔曼的原作。这幅作品中如画的风景显然受到了雅各布·鲁伊斯达尔等荷兰绘画大师的影响。

Saint Matthew is one of the twelve apostles of Jesus. The painting depicts the scene in which he was called by Jesus and became his apostle. It features impressively a thorough nature study. Its cosmological landscape dominates the epic history and makes it look like something meaningless and non-significant. The painting once decorated a chamber in Lubiąż Abbey along with missing pendant Landscape with a Hermit. Its high quality leaves no doubt that it was Willmann's work. This picturesque landscape was clearly influenced by the Dutch Masters' paintings such as Jacob Ruisdael, which distracts attention from inconspicuous biblical scene taking place in the left.

23. 圣凯瑟琳
Saint Catherine

若非画中出现的剑、车轮和棕叶等基督教元素，这幅圣凯瑟琳画像更像是在石柱和卷帘的背景下，一位身着华美庭袍、发型雍容、头戴珍珠的典型贵族女性形象。这幅画作小巧精美，展现了威尔曼的独特技巧：以红色为基调，朱砂色使其肤色红润，黑色表现衣物阴影，白色的干厚颜料增强立体感。

Although she is represented with the attributes of her martyrdom (sword, wheel, and palm), St Catherine looks like a noble court lady posing against a column and a draped curtain in her exquisite gown and sophisticated hairstyle with pearls. This small, eye-catching sketch reveals Willmann's technique: using red tones in the underpainting. Vermilion to mark complexion, black to model drapery, and dry white impastos for plasticity.

24. 圣莫妮卡
Saint Monica

这幅画中圣莫妮卡，一位悲伤的母亲正在为其子奥古斯丁不愿皈依教会而祈祷和哭泣。人们曾一度认为这幅画不是出自威尔曼之手，但是在对比这幅与另一幅卢比昂日修道院的油画《圣瓦伦蒂诺安抚男孩》后，同样使用堆积的颜料来造型的方式（类似于阿诺德·弗雷伯格的肖像画）、使用木质底板，以及相同的签名等特征都强有力地证明了这就是威尔曼的作品。其椭圆形的外框表明它原本是打算放在祭坛上的。

St Monica is praying for the conversion of her son Augustine and crying because he is unwilling to do so. The attribution of this painting was once questioned. However, a number of features strongly suggest it is Willmann's work: the characteristic way of defining form with thick smudges of paint (like in Arnold Freiberger's portrait), using a wood panel as support and an inscription betraying the same hand as in Willmann's confirmed work *St Valentine Healing a Boy* from Lubiąż Abbey. The painting's oval shape suggests that it was initially intended to be set in an altarpiece.

25. 圣乌尔苏拉
Saint Ursula

中世纪传说中，圣乌尔苏拉是不列颠岛西南部一个王国的公主，她在一万一千名童贞侍女陪同下外出朝圣，但遭到来自亚欧草原的游牧民族袭击并杀害。画作描绘了圣乌尔苏拉被弓箭射中的场景。画作构思十分素朴，人物姿势并不张扬，仅用树枝表现背景。但是画作线条粗犷，使用了大片的厚涂的油彩和明快的色彩，乌尔苏拉腰间的祖母绿绸带尤为突显。

According to medieval legend, St Ursula was the daughter of the king of in south-west Britain. The Hunter killed her in Cologne with the eleven thousand virgins who companioned her along the pilgrimage. The scene depicts the saint's death as her body is pierced with an arrow. The composition is quite modest with conventional gestures and tree branches suggesting a landscape in the background but its painterly treatment is bold, with wide impastos and vivid colours, especially the emerald green drapery around St Ursula's waist.

26. 小天使
Putti

在天使唱诗班座椅雕塑群中，施坦因尔塑造了一群热闹的大天使和小天使形象，他们演奏着各种乐器，组成了一个天堂管弦乐队。其中，小天使群像是巴洛克时期的典型形象——胖乎乎的裸身顽童前额尤为突出，他们拥有镀金的翅膀，演奏着不同的乐器，其中甚为有趣的是叉铃，这是一种由青铜或黄铜制成的响铃乐器可能来自古

埃及。为了便于固定在唱诗班座椅上，小天使上都开了小洞。

On the angelic choir stalls, Steinl sculptures a chirpy group of angels and putti playing various instruments, creating together a heavenly orchestra. The Putti are typical Baroque figures, which present as naked, chubby, impish children with unnaturally high and convex foreheads, gilded wings and stripes of drapery covering their pubes. They are playing different instruments, and one of especially interesting is the sistrum - a type of rattle made of bronze or brass, associated with ancient Egypt. All sculptures have holes that allowed attaching them firmly to the stalls.

Ⅰ 吹号小天使
Putto playing the Horn

Ⅱ 吹喇叭小天使
Putto playing the Cornett

Ⅲ 演奏提琴小天使
Putto playing the Violin

Ⅳ 吹笛小天使
Putto playing the Pipe

Ⅴ 演奏叉铃小天使
Putto playing the Sistrum

Ⅵ 演奏敲弦古钢琴小天使
Putto playing the Clavichord

27. 坐狮与小天使
Sitting Lion with a Putto

从档案图片上看，唱诗班座椅上曾有四个这样的坐狮雕塑，用来装饰座椅栏杆的转角。每个狮子都拿着卷轴，狮子上面是一个头戴花环的小天使站在后面的装饰台上。狮子抬头向上看，表情呼之欲出，似乎是因为小天使而烦扰不堪。

The archival photographs of the angelic choir stalls in situ in the abbey church in Lubiąż show the corners of the balustrades decorated with four lions. Each lion is holding a scroll and above its head a putto with a garland is propped on a bracket. The lion is looking up as if surprised and disturbed by the putto's presence.

28. 三个天使头像装饰及莨苕叶形装饰

Bracket with three angel's heads and acanthus leaves

三个天使头像装饰是用来装饰唱诗班座椅前面的挡板的。

The brackets decorated with three angel's heads used to adorn front panels of the choir stalls.

29. 贝壳图案檐口装饰及莨苕叶形装饰

Shell motif from the cornice and acanthus leaves

贝壳图案檐口装饰是每一个唱诗班座椅正上方的装饰。形状不同且排列各异的莨苕叶形装饰，为唱诗班座椅上方"小天使乐队"营造出灌木丛一样的自然环境。

Shell motifs articulated the choir stalls and adorned the upper part of each seat. Acanthus leaves in different shapes and arrangements created a dense thicket in the upper part of the choir stalls where the figures of putti with instruments were placed.

30. 贝壳图案檐口装饰及莨苕叶形装饰

Shell motif from the cornice and acanthus leaves

31. 小天使饰带一组

Friezes with Putti

这些饰带是圣白芭蕾或圣吕佳田祭坛栏杆的一部分，祭坛位于卢比昂日修道院的圣雅各布辅助教堂。这些装饰和已出版的署名为"M. Steinle dell. Wratislavia，1684"（M. 施坦因尔，弗罗茨瓦夫，1684 年）的版画中刻画的饰带几乎完全一样。此外，已定型的叶形装饰表明这属于施坦因尔晚期的作品。灵感也可能来自天使唱诗班座椅上的叶形装饰。有趣的是，创作于1713—1718 年的西里西亚耶莱尼亚古拉教堂主祭坛拥有几乎完全一样的饰带，是由托马斯·威斯菲尔德及其工坊完成的。这种现象证明了即使施坦因尔离开了西里西亚，他所设计的图案依然为人们争相模仿。

The friezes originally decorated the balustrade of the side altar of St Barbara or St Lutgardis in St James' Church in Lubiąż Abbey. At first glance, they were modeled after the friezes depicted in the series of published engravings signed "M. Steinle dell. Wratislavia 1684". However, it seems more likely that they were actually inspired by the acanthus decoration of the angelic stalls in the abbey church in Lubiąż but the ornament seems "drier" and less plastic which suggests that they were carved somewhat later. An almost identical balustrade surrounds the high altar (1713-1718) of the church in Jelenia Góra in Silesia. It was produced by Thomas Weissfeld's workshop attesting to Steinl's lasting influence in Silesia long after his departure for Austria.

Ⅰ 小天使饰带

Frieze with a Putto

Ⅱ 小天使饰带

Frieze with a Putto

32. 大卫

David

大卫是《圣经》中以色列的国王。当他还是一个年轻的牧童时，非利士人攻打以色列，大卫用投石器杀死了巨人哥利亚，使他广为人知。另外，他也因超凡的音乐和歌唱技艺闻名于世。这尊雕塑表现的就是正在演奏竖琴的大卫。《大卫》和《先知》均出自卢比昂日修道院教堂的施洗约翰祭坛。作者的灵感可能来源于树立在修道院门前的巴洛克早期风格的圣母玛利亚石柱。

David was a biblical king of Israel. He is best known for his proverbial fight with giant Goliath during the war with the Philistines. David, at the time a young shepherd, killed his powerful opponent by throwing a stone with his sling. He was also famous for his musical and singing skills. This sculpture of David is playing a harp. Both David and The Prophet come from the altar of St John the Baptist located in the ambulatory of the abbey church in Lubiąż. The sculptor was probably inspired by the statues from the early Baroque Marian column erected in front of the abbey.

33. 先知

The Prophet

34. 大天使米迦勒

Saint Michael the Archangel

在《圣经》中大天使米迦勒是众天使之首。米迦勒经常身着甲胄铁翼，以一种与化身为巨龙的撒旦搏斗的形象出现。米迦勒也会出现在最后的审判中，他手持天秤，衡量死者生前的善恶。这座雕塑来自卢比昂日修道院中圣詹姆斯教堂的主祭坛。米迦勒身着铠甲，原本握在手中的火焰之剑已经丢失了。此雕像动感极强，扭曲的身躯和被风吹起的衣物栩栩如生地表现了激烈的战斗场面。

In Christianity the Archangel Michael is the most important of all angels. He is usually depicted wearing an armour with wings, fighting Satan appearing as a dragon. Sometimes he also holds the scales to weigh good and bad deeds of the dead during the Last Judgment. This sculpture originally topped the high altarpiece of St James' Church which served as a relief chapel at Lubiąż Abbey. The Archangel Michael is shown wearing a Classical cuirassed armour but the flaming sword is missing. The statue is very dynamic, the heavenly warrior's twisted pose and windblown drapery emphasizing movement.

35. 婴儿与守护天使

Infant with the Guardian Angel

这幅画中的男婴虽然被描绘为睁着双眼，但其实这是一幅纪念夭折婴儿的画，类似一篇墓志铭。守护天使站在他的身后，引领襁褓中的婴儿去天堂，婴儿头顶上的王冠意味着他将被拯救而获得永生。周围绘有虚空派的象征物——比如容易枯萎的玫瑰与郁金香花，象征了世俗享乐和人类生活的徒劳，而石榴果实则象征着复活。

Although the baby boy is depicted as alive, with his eyes open, the painting is an epitaph commemorating a deceased infant. The Guardian Angel carrying the swaddled child to heaven raises a crown above his head in reference to the salvation of his soul and eternal life awaiting him. Among the symbols of Vanitas (futility of earthly pleasures and transience of human life on earth), the roses, the tulips (flowers prone to wilting), the pomegranate fruit, in Christian iconography symbolising the Crucifixion and Resurrection of Christ as the source of salvation.

36. 附盖罐

Can with lid

这件罐子采用金属锤揲工艺，在器物表面形成凹凸的莨苕叶形纹饰和手持弓箭的丘比特形象。

This repoussé piece is richly decorated with acanthus leaves and depictions of Cupid with bow and arrows.

37. 弥撒用器皿

Pyx

这是一件弥撒时使用的器皿，盖上是一对田园牧歌式的恋人形象，但其中更深层的内涵是指天主教会常被刻画成为基督的未婚新娘，象征着上帝和凡人之间神圣的爱。

On the lid of this utensil, which used during Mass, an idyllic scene with a pair of lovers was depicted. It has a deeper meaning though - the Catholic Church is often described as a bride betrothed to Christ to underline the divine love of God and people.

38. 弗罗茨瓦夫剪毛呢工行会葬礼铭牌

Funerary shield of the guild of cloth shearers from Wrocław

这件椭圆形铭牌中间的拱门下方有一个带有行会标志的涡形饰牌：狮鹫（格里芬）站在中间，右爪持一把刷子，左爪中的剪切机的螺旋桨组成万字符记号。饰牌上方为盔饰和垂帷及奥地利双头鹰形顶饰，鹰的胸前有一毛呢剪。拱门柱子两侧各立一女像，持十字架的代表"信仰"，持锚的代表"希望"。鹰的上方有19世纪后雕刻上去的行会名和工匠长们的铭文，最下方的椭圆形中是制作时雕刻的行会名。

In the centre of the shield, an arcade supported on two columns frames the guild's emblem set in a cartouche: the rampant griffin holding a comb in its right paw and in its left paw the screws of the shears mechanism forming a swastika. The cartouche is topped with a mantled and crested helmet: the crest renders the two-headed Austrian eagle with shears on its breast. The emblem is flanked by two personifications standing in front of the arcade's column: Faith with the cross and Hope with the anchor. Above the coat of arms the name of the guild and its masters were engraved in the 19th century and the oval below features the original inscription.

39. 弗罗茨瓦夫新城布商出师学徒兄弟会葬礼铭牌

Funerary shield of the fraternity of journeymen cloth shearers in the New Town in Wrocław

这件铭牌中间是行会标志：剪切机和交叉的梳棉机在中间，侧面是成对的梳子，起绒机以及用于在桌子固定布匹上的钩子。两侧是"信仰"（持十字架和圣杯）的化身和"希望"（持锚和隼)的化身。上方的天使持环带，上面刻着兄弟会名称。下方的另一条环带上刻有捐赠者的名字和十字腿骨的骷髅。1263年弗洛茨瓦夫的西边建立一座新城，且于1327年并入了弗罗茨瓦夫，但两城还继续保留了各自的行会。

The guild's emblem is featured in the centre: the shears and crossed carders flanked by the pairs of combs, teasel frames and hooks for attaching the cloth to the table. The border surrounding the emblem features the personifications of Faith (with the cross and chalice) and Hope (with the anchor and falcon) and above is an angel holding a banderole inscribed with the name of the brotherhood. Under the emblem is a skull with crossbones and another banderole inscribed with the names of the donors. The New Town was founded in 1263 to the west of Wrocław. In 1327 it was incorporated in the City of Wrocław but retained its separate guild organization.

40. 弗罗茨瓦夫渔夫行会葬礼铭牌

Funerary shield of guild of fishermen in Wrocław

这件铭牌上以月桂花环衬行会标志：波浪里有一艘小船，渔网铺在交叉的船桨上。下方有三条咬苹果的鱼，呈Y字形排列。

The shield features the guild's emblem set in a laurel wreath: the boat with the fishing net spread on crossed paddles, braving the waves. Below, three fish biting an apple form the letter "Y".

41. 拉齐布日钉工及铁匠行会葬礼铭牌

Funerary shield of the guild of nailers and blacksmiths in Racibórz

该椭圆形铭牌上装饰有多层葡萄藤花环，中间是行会标志：倒置的马蹄铁中间是一把锤子，上方有三枚钉子，一女性半身像在下方托起标志，标志上方是两个男性半身像手持皇冠，皇冠上有"MW"的字母缩写，可能是捐赠者的名字。

The oval shield richly decorated with grapevine wreaths showcases the guild's emblem in the centre: the horseshoe with its ends pointing downwards and the hammer between them and above the heart pieced with three nails. The emblem is supported by a female half- figure. Above the emblem, two male half-figures hold a crown inscribed with initials "MW", probably in reference to the donor.

42. 弗罗茨瓦夫制革行会葬礼铭牌

Funerary shield of the guild of whittawers and chamois-leather makers in Wrocław

这件圆形铭牌中间两名天使手持带有行会标志的涡形饰牌。行会标志上有一圆柱（将皮革脱毛、脱垢的鞣制木），左右为两把弧形刮皮刀。下方是一把用于打磨的环形刀，左右为半圆形羊皮纸刀。标志的背景是一个"W"缩写和日期。铭牌顶部刻着行会创建的铭文。

In the center of the shield, two angels hold a cartouche with the guild's emblem: the column (symbolising the tanning log on which leathers were unhaired and scudded) flanked by fleshing knives, and below is circular knife used for smoothing which flanked by round knives. The background is inscribed with the letter "W" and a date. The shield's upper section features a cartouche with the founding inscription.

43. 弗罗茨瓦夫姜饼生产者行会啤酒杯

Tankard of the guild of gingerbread makers from Wrocław

杯身上刻有行会成立的铭文，以及创始人的名字：来自卢班的克里斯托弗·里默尔。带链的杯盖上刻有棕榈叶图案。

The tankard is engraved with the founding inscription naming the donor: Christoph Riemer from Lubań. The hinged lid is decorated with a palmette motif.

44. 弗罗茨瓦夫屠夫行会锡壶

Jug of the guild of butchers in Wrocław

壶上刻着屠牛的场景。壶盖上站立着一个身披罗马军团护甲的骑士小塑像，手持涡形饰牌，上面刻有行会标志和日期。

The jug is engraved with the scene of ox slaughtering. The lid is topped by the figurine of a knight in the Roman legionary's armour holding a cartouche with the guild's emblem and a date.

45. 弗罗茨瓦夫屠夫行会杯子

Cups of the guild of butchers in Wrocław

这两件杯子外形几乎完全相同，上面刻有行会标志：两头对立的公牛，上面是一对交叉的斧子，下面是交叉的两把刀，一把普通刀，一把牛肚刀。

The pair of almost identical cups are both carved with the guild's emblem: two oxen face each other with crossed axes above them and crossed knives (a regular one and a tripe knife) below.

46. 克沃兹科染料行会酒壶

Pitcher of the dyers' guild of Kłodzko

壶体上是两只持行会标志的狮鹫，在标志上，装满植物染料的大锅和两只交叉的搅拌棒是由锤揲工艺制作而成的。

The pitcher is decorated with two griffins holding the guild's emblem: the caldron with dyeing plants inside, above it two crossed stirrers.

47. 附盖迎客杯

Wilkom with a lid

这个迎客杯上有两圈狮头装饰，狮头衔黄铜环原用于悬挂盾形吊饰，现已丢失。杯身上刻有出师学徒们的名字。杯盖上是一个身披罗马军团甲胄的骑士小塑像，手中原有涡形饰牌和旗帜，也已丢失。

The wilkom is decorated with two rows of handles in the shape of lion's heads with brass rings for attaching pendant shields. On the body of a wilkom, the names of the journeymen are engraved. On the lid stands a figurine of a knight in Roman legionary's armour that used to hold a cartouche and a banner.

48. 亚沃尔制桶工行会迎客杯

Wilkom of the guild of coopers from Jawor

这个迎客杯杯身上刻画了两名制桶工制作木桶的画面。下方是一圈狮头装饰，狮头衔铜环原用于悬挂盾形饰牌，现已丢失。杯盖上是一个身披罗马军团甲胄的骑士小塑像，手中原有涡形饰牌和旗帜，也已丢失。

On the body of a wilkom, there is an engraved scene depicting two coopers making a barrel. Below is a row of handles in a shape of lion's heads for attaching pendant shields. On the lid stands a figurine of a knight in Roman legionary's armour that used to hold a cartouche and a banner.

49. 希维德尼察石匠砖匠行会迎客杯

Wilkom of the guild of stonemasons and bricklayers from Świdnica

这个迎客杯上有两圈狮头装饰，狮头衔黄铜环原用于悬挂盾形吊饰。杯盖上是一个身披罗马军团甲胄的骑士小塑像，手握涡形饰牌上刻行会标志。

The wilkom is decorated with two rows of handles in a shape of lion's heads with brass rings for attaching pendant shields. On the lid stands a figurine of a knight in Roman legionary's armour holding a cartouche with the guild's emblem.

50. 弗罗茨瓦夫木匠和磨坊主行会迎客杯上的吊饰

Pendant shield of wilkom of the carpenters' and millers' guild in Wrocław

这块迎客杯盾形吊饰中间为一纹章，一头凶猛的狮子持柳叶刀和三角旗。上面是盔饰、垂帷和顶饰（羽饰）图案。顶饰上方伸出披甲胄，握佩剑的手臂。顶饰左右两侧刻着"MW"和"GH"缩写。

In the centre of this pendant shield is a coat of arms: the rampant lion holding a lance with a pennant, and surmounted by a mantled and crested helmet. The crest features an armoured arm holding a sword and flanked by initials "MW" and "GH".

51. 弗罗茨瓦夫篮子制作者行会迎客杯上的吊饰

Pendant shield of wilkom of the basket makers' guild in Wrocław

这个八角形的盾形吊饰中间是手持月桂花环的天使，花环里刻有行会的标志。标志的图案为刀、编筐和敲铁的锥子，左右各伴有一颗星，以及两个篮筐和一个字母H。天使翅膀下面还刻有太阳（左）和月牙（右）。花环周围刻着几个缩写和年代："GN / HM /AH/ HGW / HH /1679"可能是进献者的名字。

In the centre of octagonal pendant shield an angel holds the guild's emblem set in a laurel wreath: a knife, an awl for basket weaving and rapping iron flanked by two stars with two baskets and a large initial "H" below. Under the angel's wings sun (on the left) and crescent moon (on the right) are depicted. Engraved around the wreath are the initials (probably of the donors) and date: "GN / HM /AH/ HGW / HH /1679".

52. 破甲剑

Koncerz

破甲剑是16世纪以来铁翼骑兵使用的细长刺剑，这种剑可以最大程度的攻破护甲，直接从甲链中穿刺，或从甲胄片中刺入。但是它并不适于砍削，因为破甲剑主要是为了刺穿，因此它没有剑刃，只有锋利的剑头。剑锋的截面为三角形或圆形以增强牢固性。

Koncerz is a type of sword used by the heavy cavalry since 16th century. It is a thin and long thrusting sword, optimised to defeat body armour (either by piercing directly through mail links or by thrusting between the plates of plate armour), but not used to cut or slash. Since it was optimised for thrusting, the koncerz has no cutting edge, only a very sharp point; the blade itself is triangular or square in cross-section in order to be more rigid.

53. 破甲剑

Koncerz

54. 带子弹袋的火药罐（切申风格）

Powder flask with a bullet bag

这个火药罐是配合火器使用的，为西里西亚切申镇特有的产品。这里生产的火器和配件因其华丽的装饰闻名于世——通过镶嵌骨制或象牙、珍珠母贝、鹿角、仿珍珠玻璃等材质来展示植物、动物或狩猎场景等图案。这个火药罐一般别在枪手的腰带上或马鞍上。它的侧面是一个有开关的火药分发器，扳机清理刷和点火孔片固定在皮带上。另外，火药罐顶部连着一个皮制子弹袋。

This powder flask exemplifies the unique craft of gunsmiths operating in Cieszyn (Silesia). The locally produced firearms and accessories were highly regarded by the rich decoration. Designs were inlaid with bone (sometimes ivory), mother of pearl, horn, glass, etc. and featured characteristic plant motifs, animals, and hunting scenes. This powder flask used to be attached to a shooter's belt or a horse saddle. On its side there is a gunpowder dispenser with a stopper. A brush for lock cleaning and a touch hole pick are tied with a leather strap. A suede bullet pouch is attached to the top of the powder flask.

55. 别鲁图夫城堡前的烟花表演

Festive Fireworks Display in Front of the Castle in Bierutów

这幅版画描绘地是克里斯蒂安·乌尔里希·冯·威姆伯格公爵在别鲁图夫城堡花园中举办的一次烟火表演。画面周围的文字细致地描绘了烟花的种类和燃放时间。这些烟花美不胜收，如画面中心是维纳斯女神升座形象的烟花。

The print depicts the fireworks display organised by Duke Christian Ulrich von Wirtemberg in the gardens of his residential castle in Bierutów. All various kinds of fireworks used in this show are described in detail on the margins: many of them were truly stunning, like the enthroned goddess Venus depicted in the centre.

56. 1649年部分垮塌的弗罗茨瓦夫圣伊丽莎白教堂
St. Elizabeth Church in Wrocław structure's partial collapse in 1649

1649年，由于北侧的三根石柱倒塌，导致教堂的房顶、拱顶和墙体也一起坍塌，其内部比如讲道台、石柱和许多碑文都因此毁坏。但这并非教堂经历的第一次灾难——1529年塔顶的盔饰曾在风暴中被刮落。

The great damage happened to the roof, vaults and walls of the St. Elizabeth Church in 1649, was caused by the collapse of three northern pillars. The interior suffered as well: the pulpit, choir stalls and many epitaphs were damaged. It is not the first catastrophe that affected this church – in 1529 the tower's helmet collapsed during a windstorm.

57. 从南侧看弗罗茨瓦夫全景
Panorama of Wrocław from the south

这幅版画展现了弗罗茨瓦夫市全景，下方以文字方式标注这座城市最为重要的城市建筑。画面上方的两个人像坐在云端，手持弗罗茨瓦夫市盾徽的涡形饰牌。两对飞翔的天使手持写有圣经引文的缎带。

The print represents the vast panorama of Wrocław with the legend that identifying its most significant buildings. Above the buildings, two allegorical figures sitting among the clouds hold a cartouche with the city's municipal coat of arms. Two pairs of flying angels hold draperies inscribed with biblical quotes.

58. 波普维兹高地附近奥得河的游船
Pleasure Boat on the Oder at the height of Popowice

这幅版画可以分为四部分。主要部分是一艘华丽的游船，呈大型木制亭子的形状，上面以各种各样的塑像、植物和彩灯作为装饰。左下方是船的内饰，右侧是船的设计图。中间有画家姓名和船主信息的铭文。这艘船的主人是王权伯爵卡尔·菲利普，他是弗罗茨瓦夫采邑主教弗朗茨·路德维希的兄弟。

This print is divided into four sections of which the principal depicts the ornate pleasure boat in the form of a large wooden pavilion, richly decorated with various statues, plants, and lampions. Below, on the left, the interior of the ship is shown, and on the right is the footprint of the ship. The inscription in the middle records the names of the artists and informs the ownership of the ship to Prince Carl Philipp von Pfalz-Neuburg, the brother of Bishop of Wrocław Franz Ludwig.

59. 绘有弗罗茨瓦夫全景画的邮车时间表和价目表
Timetable and price list of postal services with panorama of Wrocław

这张时刻表在一座充满寓意装饰的建筑中。顶部为四只飞马拉着商业之神赫尔墨斯的战车。下方的扇形壁龛中巨人阿特拉斯肩负着地球，他靠在一个涡形饰牌旁，饰牌中描绘的是两个男子通过望远镜观察火焰的画面。时刻表左右为站在台柱上的两个女神形象——左边是戴安娜女神，手持大力神赫拉克勒斯的大棒，她身旁是一头鹿。右边的女像持朱庇特的一支弓箭、一束闪电和猎鹰。中下方是一块绘有弗罗茨瓦夫全景的帷幔，左右各有一个标志: 左边是飞蛾扑向燃烛，右边是一座钟。

The timetable is set into an architectural structure, which richly decorated by the complex allegorical iconography. On the top a chariot of Mercure, the god of commerce, is shown drawn by four winged horses. Below, in a scalloped niche Atlas is depicted supporting the globe and leaning on a cartouche depicting two men observing a fire through a telescope. The timetable is flanked by two female figures elevated on consoles: on the left it is goddess Diana holding Hercules' club, with a deer to her side, and the figure one on the right is shown with Jupiter's attributes: the arrow, the thunderbolt, and the eagle. In the centre of the bottom part there is drapery with a panoramic view of Wrocław flanked by two emblems: a lit candle with moths flying towards it on the left and a clock with a slanted dial on the right.

60. 奥瓦斯卡大街的客栈内景

The interior of an Inn on the Oławska Street

这幅特别的图画描绘了小酒馆内的场景, 配有服务人员和客人的行为活动解释, 例如:
A-收钱的女人
B-用酒桶倒酒的服务生
C-端啤酒的服务生
D-擦桌子的杂工
E-帮助端酒的厨师
F,G,H, I-玩各种游戏的客人
K-拿钥匙环的女房东

This unique print shows the interior of an inn with a legend explaining activities of the staff and the guests, e.g.:

A – A woman accepting payment

B – A waiter pouring beer from the barrel

C – A waiter serving beer

D – A dogsbody cleaning the tables

E – A cook helping with beer serving

F,G,H, I – Guests playing various games

K – A landlady with a key-ring

61. 从南侧看弗罗茨瓦夫全景

Panorama of Wrocław from the south

这幅版画除了全景图外还表现了商业城市财富的寓意, 象征着 "道德" (Virtue) 化身的女像手抱几支谷穗, 脚边是一个蜂巢。一群小天使拿着几捆布料, 周围散落着包裹和酒桶。城市图景上方绘有象征着神圣罗马帝国的双头鹰, 鹰爪持节杖和圆球。

The allusion complements this panoramic view to the city's wealth as a thriving center of commerce: the allegory of Virtue holding ears of corn with a beehive near her feet and putti carrying bales of cloth, surrounded by packages and barrels. Above the city view, the two-headed eagle of the Holy Roman Empire is depicted, holding a sceptre and an orb in its claws.

62. 圣抹大拉玛利亚教堂图书馆

Library at the St. Mary Magdalene Church in Wrocław

这幅画展现了哥特式晚期风格的图书馆内饰, 馆内装饰性的栏杆上是7座希腊哲学家的塑像。

The print presents the library's Late Gothic interior with a decorative balustrade topped by seven figures of Greek philosophers.

后记

首都博物馆与波兰弗罗茨瓦夫国立博物馆于 2016 年启动了两馆之间最重要的合作项目。该项目在中国驻波兰大使馆的大力支持下，实现了两馆相互引进交流展览的意愿，并签署了长期战略合作协议。

2017 年 12 月 11 日，首都博物馆成功在弗罗茨瓦夫国立博物馆举办了《晚明时期的中国人生活》展，该展通过 106 件套文物将中国 16、17 世纪明代文人生活、宗教信仰，以及繁荣的市井生活画卷展现给波兰人民。展览受到弗罗茨瓦夫市民及波兰观众的喜爱。在 3 个月的展期内参观人数达到近 3 万次。这对于只有 60 万人口的城市来说，无疑是受到了很大的关注。展览举办期间正值中国春节，两馆举办了"美美与共——中国波兰新春读城互动进行时"活动。通过网络连线，两馆馆长和两国观众互送新春祝福，相互了解两座历史悠久的城市，加深了两国人民的友谊。

2018 年是波兰独立 100 周年，也是弗罗茨瓦夫国立博物馆成立 70 周年，中波人民也即将迎来两国建交 70 周年。在这个特别的日子，我们合作举办《重生：巴洛克时期的西里西亚——波兰弗罗茨瓦夫国立博物馆馆藏精品》展，展示来自波兰的西里西亚文化，增进两国人民的相互了解与互信，具有格外重大的意义。弗罗茨瓦夫国立博物馆馆长皮奥特拉·奥施查诺夫斯基先生对此展高度重视，亲自担任策展人，独具匠心地选取了巴洛克时期西里西亚地区最具特色的绘画、雕塑，以17 世纪下半叶中欧地区波澜壮阔的历史画卷为背景，为我们带来了难得一见的欧洲艺术与文化。虽然 17 世纪下半叶的西里西亚只是欧洲历史的一个微小缩影，但它展现在我们面前的却是一个欧洲艺术的缩影。以管窥豹可见一斑，希望我们的展览可以为您打开一扇不一样的窗。祝愿中波两国人民的友谊万古长青！

Postscript

Being strongly promoted and supported by the Embassy of China in Poland in 2016, the Capital Museum of China and the National Museum in Wrocław of Poland launched one of their most significant projects to set up a program-exchange of importing and exporting exhibitions in reciprocity. The two museums also signed an agreement which laid a foundation for a long-term strategic cooperative relationship thereafter.

On December 11th 2017, Capital Museum held an exhibition of *Chinese People's Life in the Time of Late Ming Dynasty* at the National Museum in Wrocław, Poland. A vivid picture of the life of the literati, religious beliefs and, prosperous city life in the Ming dynasty during the 16th and 17th centuries was revealed through more than 106 exhibits to the audience in Poland. The exhibition was a massive success with a total of nearly 30,000 visitors in three months. It was observed that the exhibition attracted much attention in the city of Wrocław which has a total population of only 600,000. While the exhibition was taking place, during the Chinese New Year; another event hosted by both museums, called "Reading the Cities: Collaborating with Different Cultures - Sending New Year Messages Online Between China and Poland" was on. The directors of the two museums and audiences from both countries sent out Chinese New Year blessings and best wishes to each other over the internet. The event was not only an occasion for the people in understanding the extensive history of both cities of Beijing and Wrocław; it was also a great opportunity in strengthening connections and friendship between China and Portland.

2018 is the year of the 100th anniversary of Poland regaining its independence as well as the year of the 70th anniversary of the founding of the National Museum in Wrocław. Moreover, we are going celebrate the 70th anniversary of the establishment of diplomatic relations between the People's Republic of China and the Republic of Poland in 2019. In such a special occasion, it is of great significance that our two museums have been cooperating to host the exhibition of *Silesia-Rediviva: the Baroque period in Silesia - Collection of Art and Handicrafts from the National Museum in Wrocław, Poland*. Mr. Piotr Oszczanowski, the Director of the National Museum in Wrocław, has attached great importance to the exhibition, and devoted himself to the curatorial work, carefully selected the most distinctive paintings and sculptures in the Baroque era in Silesia to share the magnificent artistic accomplishments and cultural creations achieved in the second half of the 17th century. Although, we could only explore a merely small part of the entire European history from the exhibition, but the history of Silesia presents us an epitome of the European art as whole. We hope that the exhibition will assist the audience to have a glimpse into various events and occasions in history; and open up a new window through which different scenes might be viewed. Long may the friendship between the people of China and Poland last!